S0-BXZ-983

*No Boundaries
With God*

No Boundaries With God

George Derkatch

with

Jack Chamberlin

VISION HOUSE PUBLISHERS
Santa Ana, California 92705

NO BOUNDARIES WITH GOD

Copyright © 1975 by George B. Derkatch
Toronto, Ontario M6P 3J9, Canada
Library of Congress Catalog Number 75-24674
ISBN-088449-051-3 (paperback)
All rights reserved. No portion of this book may be used in any form without the written permission of the author, with the exception of brief excerpts in magazine articles, reviews, etc.
Printed in the United States of America.

CONTENTS

FOREWORD

What would it be like if you couldn't pick up your Bible and read it? What would you do if you were forbidden to pray and were told "There is no God?" How would you like to see your church padlocked or turned into a museum?

This is actually happening right in our day and age in certain countries of the world. While science puts man on the moon and makes great medical strides, millions of people retreat into a godless realm of cruelty and hardship.

There is an organization doing something about this, and it is called World Christian Ministries. Its founder, the Reverend George Derkatch, is the author of this book, and his story tells what is being done today about this atheistic oppression.

World Christian Ministries is serving people in the United States, Canada, and the United Kingdom who want to help those behind the Iron Curtain. WCM's record is spotless and its progress is phenomenal. Thousands of Bibles are being sent each month into atheistic countries, and the tangible help they are providing is inestimable.

I endorse this book, its author, and World Christian Ministries!

> Jim Neale
> President, *Christ is the Answer*
> Toronto, Canada

INTRODUCTION

One of the most exciting things ever to happen to me was when I was asked to help in the writing of this book. Knowing the work God called Rev. George Derkatch into, and having seen it in operation for a considerable amount of time, I really feel privileged to be a little part of it.

Many times I have been in the offices of World Christian Ministries and have seen bundles of foreign Bibles being prepared to be shipped overseas. At the presses I have seen gospel literature and song books being prepared in the Slavic languages, and although I couldn't read a word of it, my heart was thrilled to know that the Word was going out to the hungry and deprived.

Many times we as Christians are concerned about physical food being sent to those in need, but there is a far greater need—and that is for spiritual food. As millions of dollars are being spent on food for the starving (and we agree 100 percent with this), there is far too little being done about that great spiritual hunger. If we do not do something about it, our world will be in far worse shape than it already is.

If you could see the letters coming into World Christian Ministries from these many countries, and the pleas they contain to send the Word, you would better understand the need. The best part of it is that every letter is taken care of, and great sacrifice is made by Brother Derkatch to fulfill this mission.

I know that on many occasions George Derkatch will make personal sacrifices so that needs among our Slavic brethren can be met. He sees, knows, and understands these people and has proven that the Communist curtain can be penetrated by the Word of God.

Every bit of this story is true, though it is sometimes hard to understand what man will do when he does not know the living God. Yet it is wonderful to see just what a man does who knows God! You'll read all about it in the pages of this book.

Jack Chamberlin

Chapter 1

An Early Start

In the beginning God created. . . .
—Genesis 1:1

It was good to be back in Toronto again, though I never looked forward to the stack of mail that always awaits my return from meetings across the country. I was especially pleased with the attendance and response in Los Angeles, and I noted particular interest in all meetings concerning the work that is so dear to my heart, reaching beyond the manmade barriers of Iron Curtain countries with the Word and other vital needs.

Helen, my secretary, had done her usual efficient job of answering whatever mail she could, carefully stacking the rest in a neat pile on my desk. "The letter you've been waiting for has arrived," she said, pointing to a rather bedraggled piece of paper on which miles of travel had taken its toll. My heart leaped when I saw the signature, for at long last here was word from Brother L!

Tears filled my eyes as I read its contents. The letter said, "Upon my arrival in Nakhodka, the customs came on board. With some they were very strict. With others they asked them whether or not they had any religious literature. With

me . . . nothing! I was cleared in minutes. Halle-
lujah!

"It was very difficult to locate the building, as
I had not received the address. According to the
map, I pinpointed what I thought to be the
church with its surrounding green fence. I literally walked up to the church! I communicated with
the caretaker's wife and could see the light of
Jesus in her eyes.

The next afternoon I went with the literature
to the church. The caretaker and his wife were
working in the garden. We quickly went inside
and sat down. As I unloaded the 51 books they
started to cry. He kissed me the real Russian way
and we praised the Lord. That evening I attended the midweek service, where approximate-
ly eighty were gathered. I saw that the literature
was handed out, though no one knew from where
or when it had come. I was just a tourist to them.
The next day I flew back home praising the
Lord!"

"This is going to be a good week," I thought as
I scanned the other mail, still rejoicing in the
news which this first letter brought. Though it
had taken several months to find out if this operation would be successful, I now sat with confirmation on my desk. And this is just one of several
letters that cross my desk each week which prove
that God is supreme, overruling man's laws that
contravene His.

"What ever got me involved in this type of
work?" I asked myself as I sat back in my chair.
It was probably the last thought in our neighbors' minds back in my home town of Glendon

(just 150 miles from Edmonton, Alberta) that one of the Derkatch boys would become a Bible smuggler.

Dad and Mom Derkatch had immigrated to Canada from the Ukraine and had settled on a farm there several years before. The farm was our birthplace, all eight of us children, and both Mom and Dad seemed pleased that their family was equally divided, four boys and four girls.

Everybody loved Dad, and although he was very strict, we respected him for it. We had long since learned that if he promised us something, he was true to his word. Many a time I tried to talk him out of a licking, but nothing moved him —if he said it, he meant it!

We always went to church, though we dreaded having to get ready on Sundays to make the long trip there, where we would line up as a family and sit on hard pews through what seemed a long and unexciting ordeal. But Dad insisted, so we had no choice.

Even though I hadn't started school, I could see that Dad didn't like church any more than the rest of us, but, being of strict European heritage, he was faithful in this custom that had been handed down from family to family. But one day there was a change . . . a man came into our area with a Bible under his arm. It wasn't long before he was holding meetings in various homes, and Dad and Mom were invited to one of them. Something happened to Father, and he came home a changed man. We couldn't understand it, but now he took time to pray and talk to God, and it seemed like he knew Him. Mother was different too, and although we didn't dare talk about it, there was no doubt we were all wondering.

Now we stopped going to the big church up the road on Sundays, and instead the Derkatch family went to a little meeting place over on South Road. And each Sunday that same preacher was there with his Bible under his arm.

We didn't mind going to church as much now, because this man was exciting to hear. He kept telling us that God was alive and had sent His Son Jesus for us. In a very persuasive manner he would urge us to accept Jesus Christ as our Savior and let Him live in us. My brothers and sisters seemed to understand what he was talking about and soon, like Dad and Mom, there was a change in their lives.

I guess I must have been too young to really understand, for I was the last one to give in. And then it wasn't until the day my father took me aside and said, "George, you've got to get saved! Get down on your knees and ask Jesus to take your sins away and come into your heart." Whatever Dad said we did without question, so I got down on my knees and began praying. I told Jesus about the times I had been bad and especially about the day I threw a stone at old Turk, our Thanksgiving turkey. I didn't know the barn window was right behind him and he'd duck as the stone went past. Jesus heard all my problems in a few short minutes, and as I got up off my knees, tears streamed down Dad's cheeks. It was the first time I had seen him softened, and I could understand why, because I was experiencing in my life the same power that had changed his!

Although I was in kindergarten when I accepted Jesus as my personal Savior, this decision was to alter the whole course of my life. Through my school years, while other kids became involved in worldly things, there was a power that was directing me another way. There was no doubt about it, God had plans for me, and although I wasn't to know fully what they were for some time, I appreciated the love and desire He placed in my heart.

Chapter 2

The New Way

Jesus said, "I am the way. . . ."
—John 14:6

L ife on the farm improved as God took His rightful place in our lives. The leadership and example was set by Dad, who lived as best he could from the Word of God, always keeping it before us as a guide and precept. The whole community respected his honesty, and I can say that never once in my presence or to my knowledge did he ever lie.

There were conflicting times, though, especially in harvest season. We would work hard in the fields to get the crops in, but when it came to prayer night and church time, everyone set aside their tools and went to church. There was no excuse for missing services, and many a time even though ideal harvesting weather didn't reach us until a Sunday, the whole family would still set aside all work to honor God's day of rest. Frequently my older brothers would become concerned about the crops because Dad insisted that they stop for church services on Sundays instead of taking advantage of the good weather, but never once would Dad allow us to work instead of worship. And God honored his faith, for not one crop or sheaf of grain was lost because of bad weather. We were to learn that Dad even expected the horses to rest when worship time came around, and when he closed them into the barn there was no way we could change his mind. I am thankful for this example and heritage which Dad gave me, for I am sure it is influential in the work I am involved in today.

The Great Depression hit the West badly, and it was almost impossible to eke out a living for our family of eight on the farm. Stories came from the East that people were finding work in the big cities and were even able to get homes for their families. One morning Dad broke the news to Mom and the rest of our family. We were selling the farm and moving East. What was Dad going to do for a living in eastern Canada? Our only reply was that "God is still Master of this home, and He has special plans for us there."

In a small community word travels fast, and soon strangers were coming to the farm. Private conversations were held with Father as he took these people across the flat meadows and through our storm-beaten and aging buildings. We were not anxious to hear the results of these meetings, for we expected sooner or later to hear that the farm was sold and we'd be moving. When you've lived in a certain place all your life, you become attached to it, and leaving is like parting from a dear friend.

But the inevitable had to come, and one day Dad announced that, even though he couldn't sell the farm because of the depression, we were moving anyway! Our emotions were mixed, but in spite of the fact that we were leaving the homestead, there was a curious air of expectation within us.

There were many people around when we held our auction sale. Some came from curiosity, while others knew it was their last chance to say good-bye. Still others came realizing that with farm machinery and household articles being auctioned off, there could be some good buys in these hard times. As young people we enjoyed the excitement and attention of the day, and it wasn't until nightfall that we realized the real significance of it all. Our farm was gone, and now even our belongings. All that remained was what we could take on the train. That night we stayed on a neighboring farm, and the next morning as we made our way to the railroad station we caught our last glimpse of our former home.

Excitement and tears filled the air as the big steam engine puffed into the railroad station. In a fury of steam and cinders, quick good-byes were said and our few suitcases were put on board. I don't know if I liked saying good-bye, as it was really a new experience, but during the last few days I said it many times. This spoke to me of the friendship which Father had cultivated over his years in Canada.

At last the conductor herded us on board, and Father led Mother and the seven remaining children to the wooden seats in the passenger car. The train lurched forward, and we were on our way to new adventures, a new home, and a new way of life.

Traveling by train wasn't all it was put up to be, and soon we learned of the discomfort as we tried to stay on those slippery seats. We couldn't afford the luxuries of a Pullman or suite car, so these seats became our traveling home for the next several days.

It was interesting at first to watch the prairies roll past our windows, but as the hours and days rolled on, our young and active minds sought more interesting things to attract them. Hours were then spent imagining what was awaiting us at the end of our journey and how we would fit in to our new way of life.

All during the long trip eastward Father continued the leadership of his family, and although we were traveling on a public conveyance where many eyes were focused on this adventurous Ukrainian family, he still took time to instruct us in the Word of God. Our family altar was set up right in that passenger car, and every day the whole family participated. I'm sure that many other passengers heard for the first time the glorious message of Jesus Christ through Dad's booming voice as he read to us and prayed while we traveled. Though I didn't want to admit it, I knew at this time that our trip eastward would be a definite stepping-stone for me and a move in the direction God wanted me to go.

It was not surprising that there was excitement in the morning, for we woke up to see something other than flatlands out the windows. Our kindly conductor told us we were just getting through the prairies of Manitoba and would soon be into the Province of Ontario, where we were to make our new home. The next night we hardly slept, for we knew that the following morning we would be pulling into Union Station in downtown Toronto.

Finally the time arrived, and our train edged its way into the huge ornate building. Soon we were stepping off the train onto the huge concrete platform which reached alongside each set of tracks. People were hurrying from one place to another, and baggage was being whisked to and fro. We almost needed a map to get out of the place! What a change from the little station where we had climbed on board this train a few days earlier!

Relatives were on hand to meet us, and we went out onto the city street, where there was a waiting car. What a far cry from the quiet, peaceful prairie farm we had left behind! Everywhere I looked there were buildings, and it seemed as if they reached the sky! I was sure I would miss the vast expanse afforded the prairie dweller and those grain elevators which would loom in the distance on a clear summer night. This was to be our new home, though, and we resolved to get used to it.

Soon Father and brothers found work, and we were moving into a little home. This was welcome, for we spent several weeks separated while Dad found work and a place to live. Relatives and friends had been gracious in making our presence in this new city welcome.

Coming together again, Father was quick to give thanks to God for all that He accomplished in the past short while. Now we were to settle down to a brand new way of life, with Dad and older brothers working in factories while my younger sisters and myself were quickly settling into new schools.

The city schools were quite different from the country ones we had attended, and I was sad to see that I would be separated from my sisters. Each grade had its own classroom, whereas in the previous school all classes were held in one room. The new school was nice, though, for the teachers had more time for us and made learning more interesting. I was now determined to get a good education so that some day I could become a prosperous and successful businessman.

Adapting to city life wasn't all that bad, for we had so many things we didn't have before. Months slipped into years, and it wasn't long before I graduated from high school. My part-time job turned into a full one when I left school, but it seemed that there was more in life for me. In fact, it was at this point that I knew God was calling me into the full-time ministry, though I didn't want to accept it.

A friend had been working in a lumber camp up north, and on one of his trips down he told me of the easy money to be made up there. Here was a great way to escape God's call and raise money to become a beef rancher! I decided to resign my job and go north for a couple of years. Then my friend and I would together become partners in a ranch.

But God had different plans, and in spite of our reasoning that with wartime beef shortages fast money would be ours, He was about to change my mind. One morning in early spring it rained, causing ice to form on the streets. While

I was driving down the block a milk wagon cut in front of me. My brakes were worthless on the ice, and there was a loud crash! I totaled the wagon and did considerable damage to another vehicle as well as my own.

All told, it would take over two thousand dollars to put these vehicles back in their original order and, even though the wagon was on my side of the street, I was found guilty of careless driving. I thought I was going to have to go to jail. In desperation I turned to the Lord and cried, "God, get me out of this mess, and I'll go to Bible college!"

Things began to happen, and within a few days a Christian friend came and offered to fix things up. He had a body shop and suggested that we start on the other car first. It wasn't long before it was looking like new, so we called the owner. He came to look at it and took it out for a test drive, and when he returned he was willing to sign a release stating that he was satisfied. As he left my friend told me I owed him nothing and that he would start on my car right away. What seemed to be a tremendous hurdle had become a simple miracle for God, and the next thing I knew my car was on the road again, and all I had to pay was three hundred dollars! Now I was willing to answer the call and go to Bible college.

My brother Michael was pleased to hear my decision. He had already felt the call to the ministry and was preparing himself. It was encouraging to know that another member of his family was doing the same thing.

Going to Bible college was not easy, for though Dad loved God he couldn't see why I should go there. With five dollars in my pocket and his rather doubtful blessings, I was on my way. At that time the college was on Euston Street in Toronto, but because I couldn't afford to travel I got a part-time job to put me through college. I often think back on the many ways God miraculously met needs, making it possible for me not only to graduate but also to go on to Winnipeg for postgraduate work.

Chapter 3

The Call

I have called thee by thy name....
—Isaiah 43:1

Many times during my college years and even before I had heard about missionary work overseas. The more I heard about it the more interested I became, especially in eastern Europe, where my beloved Slavic people were located. Missionaries who had spent many years there preaching the gospel would bring us terrifying news about severe persecution of believers and how these faithful people stood firm for God, some even to death.

I knew God was calling me into work in eastern Europe, and I had a great desire to go over there and start meetings with the Christians. My first contact came in 1943, when I was still in my teens, with a missionary society from eastern Europe.

When World War Two began, doors for Christian work in eastern Europe gradually closed, forcing the society to transfer its operation to Canada, where many Slavic people had immigrated. Becoming a part of their organization was a great step in the plans God had for me.

Meanwhile, overseas, Slavic refugees were gathering in crowded camps, especially in Germany, and by the middle of 1945 there were more than half a million people in these camps! By the end of the war faithful believers and missionaries began the work of infiltrating these camps, and through their preaching of the Word literally thousands found Christ as their personal Savior.

My heart ached for these people, and I prayed constantly that God would give me the opportunity of working personally among them. Little did I realize how the Lord was going to work this out!

There was an air of intrigue as the director of our society approached me one day. "Brother George," he said, "you have been watching with interest the situation in eastern Europe. We are getting hundreds of requests from people who want to immigrate to Canada. Government regulations require someone to sponsor them. This is a tremendous opportunity to reach these poor souls for Christ and rescue them from the drastic situation they are now in. The Society has made arrangements with the Canadian government to send representatives overseas to assist anyone who would like to come to Canada. The person who goes will be in personal contact with these people, observing their backgrounds and assisting them in whatever way possible. I am sure many people will find the Lord if this is done as God would lead. We have met and have decided that the person we would like to send is you. Would you consider going?"

My heart leaped with joy. I could hardly believe what he was saying, and already my mind was racing forward to the work that I would be doing as I gave him my reply that I was willing to go. "You realize there is a terrific responsibility attached to this job," he continued, "for decisions as to who comes to our country will rest upon your shoulders. Also, although the war is over, there is still a certain amount of unrest and danger involved." I could not see anything except being able to fulfil the task I knew God had laid upon my heart sometime before, so I was quick in assuring him I felt I was able to do the job.

Shortly after this, arrangements were made for me to fly to Europe, where a good portion of my time during the next few years would be spent. It seemed that the plane would never reach its destination, and eager anticipation welled up in me as we flew eastward.

Upon arriving on the Continent I traveled by train over a countryside that showed the ravages of war. Scars of bombed-out factories marred the scenery, though hardy people expressed a hope that their countries would be renewed and rebuilt now that the war was over. For the next six months I was to spend my time between Hamburg and Munich. Arrangements were made so that I could conduct gospel meetings in camps where Slavic people had congregated, and during that time several hundred came to Christ.

Everywhere I went, stories came from behind the Iron Curtain about the Christian work there. Although Russia had been allies with us during the war and it looked like Christians were going to be given a chance again now that the war was over, the caustic fingers of Communism were reaching across the country's vast expanse, removing whatever religious liberty had been regained and meting out severe persecutions to the Christian believers. News came from towns and villages that churches were being closed and believers were being forced to worship underground. Bibles were seized by the hundreds and destroyed in an all-out attempt to destroy faith in God in this atheistic country. Family after family told how certain of their members were whisked away by secret police, with many of them suffering the agony of not knowing whether they were still alive or not. Others could personally show scars of severe beatings by police as they attempted to get these believers to deny Jesus Christ.

I talked to hundreds of men, women, and young people who refused to return to their own homeland. Terror filled their voices as they told me death was awaiting them if they returned. Although opportunities were there daily to go back home, seldom did anyone take them, and some, in fear of being forced back, even committed suicide rather than returning home. The picture was very clear, especially for those who chose to serve Jesus Christ instead of the dictates of their godless government. It meant becoming third-class citizens under severe persecution, possible imprisonment for any trivial reason, deprival of work, and possible starvation. How could we encourage these people to return home?

While I was in Germany many refugees told of the great need for Slavic gospel literature,

31

such as song books, tracts, food, and clothing. Persecuted Christians were looking to the free countries for help. As Christian brothers we could not stand idly by, and as more shared this need with me I saw that something had to be done and done quickly.

On returning home from this first European missionary venture I shared this great need to the people in our churches. The response was very favorable, and a Slavic literature program was started in Edmonton. By 1950 we had published our first gospel tract, and through good friends in South America we were able to buy many Russian and Ukrainian Bibles and song books to send to these people. The cry from eastern Europe echoed over and over—"Send us God's Word that we may believe!" There was no doubt that the efforts of the Communist governments were reasonably successful in destroying the Word which believers looked to for spiritual encouragement and help. "How can a person believe if he hasn't heard?" I thought, "and how can he hear if there are no Sacred Scriptures for him to have?"

How often this was confirmed to my heart in numerous incidents during my first visit to Germany. One time I was talking with one of our Ukrainian ministers. Offering him money that he might feed and clothe his family, he refused, saying instead, "Dear brother, thank you for your kindness, but please send us some Bibles and other gospel literature first. Our spiritual needs are far greater than our physical needs." His earnest plea touched me deeply and impressed upon my heart the great need there was.

A short while later I was in contact with another Christian brother, who related this experience to me: "When I first arrived in Germany I didn't know anyone. The loneliness was tremendous, and I prayed earnestly that God would send a Christian brother my way. When I did meet one on the street for the first time, I wept for joy and thanked God for sending a Christian my way." He assured me that these had been the most precious moments of his life.

Trainloads of people were by now going back to their homeland (much against the wishes of those involved), and one day I met a young lady who had a terrifying story to tell. With many others she had been forced to return home. As the train loaded with boxcars of unwilling passengers arrived at its destination, she managed to hide in a dark corner of the boxcar she was in. Her absence went undetected, and for several days, in spite of bitterly cold weather and a lack of food, she huddled in this hiding place. Finally the empty train was returned to Germany for another load of unfortunate people. On arrival she slipped from her moving hiding place into a new world of freedom. Many others tried the same thing, but several were detected, and death came to some through exposure to the severe weather conditions.

As my work continued among these people, I frequently had requests by weeping mothers, fathers, and even wives to search for other members of their families who were missing. Several times I had the privilege of making contact with relatives and friends, and on many occasions I was able to give them much-needed financial assistance. Other incidents were not as encouraging, especially one day when a man tearfully related this story to me: during the war his wife, whom he deeply loved, was arrested in Russia and deported to Germany. In spite of efforts to contact her, he obtained no success, and so finally he escaped to Germany himself to search for her. In the meantime his wife, not wanting to remain in Germany without him, had returned to Russia. With the end of the war she couldn't return to Germany, and now he was unable to go back to Russia. Although I could not bring about a reunion for them, I was able to assist this man financially so that he could buy clothing to send to his wife.

By now immigration was getting into full swing, and several thousand families were moving to Canada, the United States, and other free countries. In Toronto my brother Michael was pastoring a fairly large Ukrainian church. His duties brought him in contact with many of these new Canadians. It was evident that he was facing a severe handicap, for none of them could read English, and he had nothing to give them in their own language. The only logical solution was to bring gospel tracts and song books in Ukrainian as well as other Slavic languages.

Steps were made in this direction as he offered part of the church building for this great work, and thus came the birth of Christian Mission Publishers (now World Christian Ministries). With a need for Slavic literature in Canada and a great need for it overseas (especially behind the Iron Curtain), with some type of printing facilities we could produce this much-needed literature. Brethren back home were challenged by the idea, and steps were taken to buy a printing press. This was not an easy step because we didn't have any money to start with, but the Lord was in control. We formed a board of six men who, challenged by the need, took up an offering toward the new project. Altogether the offering amounted to fifteen dollars, a far cry from what was actually needed. That same day a lady from the United States gave me fifty dollars toward the work, so now we had 65 dollars toward the printing press, but that was a long way from what was actually needed to get things going.

Discouraged, I was almost convinced that it wasn't the Lord's will to continue at this time. But brother Michael felt differently! He was so convinced that this was of God that he was willing to sacrifice in order to purchase the press and get this work underway. Putting action to his vision, he approached a Christian businessman and encouraged him to invest a thousand dollars in this work. Then, after much prayer, he went to a bank and borrowed a thousand dollars in his own name, which he also invested in the project. It was a happy day when we installed the press in a small printing shop which he and a friend bought next to the church. Shortly the press was humming, and Slavic gospel literature was being produced. This was 1957, and World

Christian Ministries had begun the task of producing Christian literature for Slavic people here and abroad. Three objectives were decided upon at that time and are still being fulfilled today: (a) to translate all available gospel material into Slavic languages; (b) to send Bibles, tracts, and gospel literature free of charge to all countries in the world, especially countries in the Soviet Union; and (c) to assist all Slavic people in any way possible in promoting radio programs and missionary and relief work.

As we moved forward for the Lord in this work, progress seemed slow at first. This was mainly because of the lack of funds, but soon God was blessing this work in such a way that much Slavic literature was being produced, with all glory going to God.

As demand increased for this literature and the work load increased for my brother and myself, we soon realized that we were rapidly coming upon another major decision with this work. The burden of looking after the printing of the literature was becoming more than we could carry, and yet the distribution of this literature, the raising of funds, and the pastoring of a newly founded English-speaking church all loomed over us. We needed the Lord's direction in the matter and sought Him continually for several days. The pressures were becoming terrific, and there was no doubt that they were taking their toll on both of us. My heart was in the overseas gospel work, and I knew Michael had a tremendous burden for his new church.

You can't come before the Lord without expecting an answer, and soon it was evident what He wanted us to do. First, we were to sell the printing firm to a group of interested Christian businessmen who would carry on the duties of printing and producing needed materials. This in turn would free us from the tremendous work load there and give us time to spend on other demanding projects. The Lord then instructed us that I was to move into the gospel literature work exclusively, while Michael would continue as pastor of the church. Now I could see that the Lord had opened the door to continued work behind the Iron Curtain, where I was to continue until the Lord called Michael home.

Going into the Iron Curtain countries in 1957, when I took my first trip there, was no easy task. Unlike today, our Canadian government was not able to protect anyone visiting these countries, and a warning of this risk was stamped on our passports.

Before entering an Iron Curtain country I would have to register in our Canadian embassy in a country bordering eastern Europe. As soon as I arrived there I would have to go to the Canadian or British embassy or consulate in that country and register again. It was a repeat performance when I was ready to leave, since I first had to notify them I was going home and, as soon as I was back in the Western world, contact was made with our Canadian embassy advising them of my return.

There were many "tricks of the trade" to be learned, and a friend who had considerable experience in traveling through these countries consented to come along with me on my first trip. Our first task was to contact believers, and, because he had worked there before the war as a missionary, his able assistance proved to be invaluable. The war had made its changes, though, and we encountered great difficulty in finding Christians. Religious persecution had become so severe that we couldn't ask for any information regarding Christians, not even for a name. Divulging our mission into the country could result in imprisonment to those we came in contact with, and possibly even death. We were soon to realize that we were on our own and could depend only on the help of our Lord, who had called us into this country.

As we drove through the country we entered several towns and villages. Prayerfully we scouted the areas looking for possible leads to Christians. Then we came to one village where my friend told me he was sure some Christians lived. "We'll drive slowly," he told me, "so perhaps we may recognize someone in the village." Proceeding carefully, we noticed a large barn not far from the rough road. Suddenly the door flew open and a middle-aged woman came out carrying an armful of wood for her kitchen stove. Looking our way, and probably wondering why our car was proceeding at such a slow speed, she recognized the face of my friend. At the same time he recognized her and, as she dropped the wood and started running for the house, my friend hit the car brakes. I almost went through the windshield, and as I rubbed my head he explained to me that God had answered our prayers, for there was our first Iron Curtain Christian. "I distinctly remember that woman," he continued, "when I was called to this area before the war! She was one of a large family that were so faithful to the work of God!" As we recovered ourselves, the woman came running out with her husband. There was joy and tears in his eyes as he welcomed us. God had led us directly to the Christian leader of the village! We quickly pulled our car off the road, and as we did the man's wife opened the large barn door and we drove right inside. As soon as we were in the door was shut and locked.

This was a Saturday night, and only minutes after our arrival young people were running in every direction. I wondered what they were doing, and soon I learned that they were spreading the news of our arrival, which was to result in the house being filled with people within the next hour.

Hunger and eager anticipation marked the faces of those people as we were called upon to preach. We would preach for an hour or so and then stop, but the people would cry out to us, "Tell us more!" How can you stop when here is such a hunger for the gospel of Jesus Christ? So we continued on into the late hours of the evening. Not a single person left, and several times through the evening others arrived and squeezed into the already-crowded room. Finally we had to quit, for the night was almost over, and soon people were slipping quietly back into the protection of darkness to make their way home.

After the last ones had left, our friendly host

and hostess gave us a welcome cup of tea and sandwiches. We then went to our respective resting places, mine being in the attic of that building.

Chapter 4

The Challenge

And I sought for a man among them, that should make up the hedge and stand in the gap before me for the land. —Ezekiel 22:30

I found it hard to go to sleep that night with the excitement of what God was already doing here. Realizing that tomorrow would be another busy day for Jesus, I claimed the word of the Psalmist, who said, "He giveth his beloved sleep" (Psalm 127:2b), and shortly I dropped into a peaceful rest.

The next thing I knew, long rays of bright, early-morning sunshine were reaching across the room and onto the bed where I was sleeping. From outdoors came a murmur that I found impossible to distinguish. Jumping from my bed, I rushed to the windows overlooking the back yard. To my amazement there were hundreds of people milling around there, and inside the hall, which had been prepared for a morning meeting, there was no longer a place to sit or stand.

Dressing as quickly as I could, I rushed downstairs, where someone led me through the crowds and into the building, where an empty pulpit was awaiting my arrival. A stir of excitement swept across the crowd as we entered, and then a holy hush engulfed the whole throng. My watch indicated just a few minutes before eight o'clock that morning, and here I was preaching again! Hungry people wept as I shared the living Word of God with them, and, although I would try to stop, they interrupted with shouts of "Give us more, please give us more!" After about three hours of preaching that morning, local officials dismissed the crowd and brought me back into the house, where I could partake of some food and refreshment for my body. Even as I was finishing a meal that I knew was prepared with love and sacrifice by these people, I could sense that many were gathering outside again.

"Brother Derkatch, you must preach to us again this afternoon," a Christian leader pleaded. "Word has traveled among our people, and they are gathering by the hundreds to hear more of God's Word," he continued, "and we must not let these people return without hearing from our Canadian Christian friend." Seeing the sincerity of this plea and the spiritual hunger of these people, I knew that God wanted us to stay, and so by two o'clock they were ushering me back into the pulpit again as several hundred more waited to be fed the Word of God.

As in the morning service, if there was any indication that I was going to stop preaching, they would plead for me to continue. There was no doubt that God was working among these people, for from these weary and worn faces came tears as the Word went forth. God was speaking to hearts, and several who had never known Jesus were brought to a saving knowledge of Him before this meeting ended shortly after five in the afternoon.

It wasn't long before the darkness of night had crept in, and I was given the privilege of moments for prayer before another meal was served. I joined with the brethren to partake, and several of them, I learned, were representatives of different underground churches. They came in from various outlying areas so they could be refreshed from the Word and bring this back to their people. Many of them told me during the supper hour that their people would be coming at the risk of being caught and persecuted by police and government officials. But they would come anyway in order to be part of the evening meeting which was now being planned. It amazed me that in such an atheistic country word traveled so rapidly and that such great crowds could gather at short notice for a Christian meeting. This was done without the aid of modern advertising such as we have in America or Canada. "Oh," I thought, "If only we could let the people back home see how these deprived ones are so faithful and hungry for God!"

Equally as many were on hand for this night service as had been present for the previous two. Already I had preached over six hours that day, so during the night service we took turns preaching for almost six hours. Again the people never tired of hearing the Word of God, and, although it was very late when we finished and some had to travel several miles under darkness, they still wanted us to continue. Knowing that our physical bodies could stand only so much, we felt it wise to dismiss them and get some much-needed rest.

44

There were tea and sandwiches awaiting us when we returned to the home of our host and hostess. Some stayed to eat and fellowship with us for those few precious moments left. As we ate I was disturbed about something I had noticed among the hundreds of people I had seen that day. It was a shocking sight, and I couldn't believe my eyes, for among them all there had not been a single Bible, hymnbook, or other piece of Christian literature. Many people throughout that day had come to me asking for Bibles. Their cry was "Help us get Bibles and hymnbooks so we can continue to learn and worship the Savior!"

Being disturbed about this shocking revelation, I asked some of the Christian leaders who were still with us why there was such a scarcity of Christian literature, song books, and Bibles. "Surely churches must have this literature from even before the days of Communism?" I asked. Then came the startling revelation—churches were without Christian literature, Bibles, and song books! One brother told me, "When the Communist government took over our country, an all-out effort was made to rid the country of any literature that spoke of God. Although the outside world thinks we have a certain amount of freedom to worship, this is not true, and, except for churches in areas where tourists travel, the only Christian literature of any type that we have is what we have been able to hide from the authorities or produce by hand." At that moment, seeing firsthand the conditions, I knew that God wanted us in the free world to do something about this situation, for everywhere I turned there was someone asking me for Bibles. As a matter of fact, several people just that day had asked me if they could have my own Bible. Before going to sleep that night, I got down before God and prayed that He would use me in every way possible to set up an organization which would effectively supply Bibles and other Christian literature to our Christian brethren in these deprived countries.

Early the next morning the leader of the believers awoke us and told us that, because of the vast crowds which had accumulated for meetings the day before, he had received word that secret police would be carrying out an investigation. His informant said this would begin at 7 A.M., "so you must be on the way long before they get here," he continued, "and we have already made arrangements and there is a car ready to lead you on to the next place. We will see that you get there safely, and word has gone ahead, so the believers are expecting you."

"How wonderful God works!" I thought, remembering that as we arrived in this country we didn't even know where to go or who to see. Now God had not only led us to the Christian believers but had provided people who could put us in touch with still other believers. But, after all, isn't that just what the Bible says in Philippians 4:19: "My God shall supply all your needs according to his riches in glory by Christ Jesus." We had been so well taken care of, and now it seemed that God was giving us a human ring of protection and direction.

A breakfast of good staple food was awaiting us when we went downstairs. Quickly we ate, noting the air of urgency among the people, and in the shadow of darkness we moved into the early morning to find that they had already prepared our car, having removed it from the barn, and another vehicle was standing by to lead us on.

Although the roads are not like our Western roads, and it is necessary to proceed with reasonable caution if we don't want to shake our car and ourselves to pieces, we were still several kilometers from where we started when the morning sun cast its long rays from the east and started to provide the morning light. The only traffic we saw was the occasional bicycle and a couple of military vehicles, but it was evident that farm workers were well underway, for we could see them going to and fro from their farm buildings and fields.

It was still reasonably early in the day when we arrived at our first destination, which was about 400 kilometers from where we began. Word had already gone ahead, and there was another group of believers awaiting our arrival.

Our instructions had been to proceed straight into the town, and when the lead car turned left, we continued for two blocks and then turned right. Obeying these instructions, we parked the car and walked one block down to the house with a fence and gate. As we walked up the steps I heard a man say "O.K.", and the door was quickly opened and we were ushered in. I was surprised to see one of the brethren from the first

47

place we visited standing there. Apparently he had gone ahead during the night so he could be with the believers when we arrived. This afforded him the opportunity to identify us, as he had seen us before and would recognize our faces. Each person as he came to the door was identified before he was allowed to enter. Then the door opened quickly and he slipped in. This was a safeguard against any intrusion from the secret police.

As I mentioned before, many believers were waiting for us, and, as we were directed down a set of stairs and into a rather dark basement, I could see that it was already filled with people. Two lights were hanging, one in each end of the room, and, although it was now light outside, they had to be on, for the basement room had only one small window to let in the outdoor light.

"Preach, Brother," I was told as a brother led me to the front of the room. So without any preliminaries I began to preach. Tears streamed down the cheeks of the believers as I preached and shared the Word of God. Although we are sometimes led to believe that the only believers left in Communist lands are the aged and infirm, I was soon to learn differently. For in all the meetings so far there was a large number of young people who were willing to take the great risk to worship the living God. There was a great stir among the people, and when I concluded my message there was evidence that several accepted Jesus Christ as their own Savior.

None of the believers moved as we left the room. A brother instructed us to go immediately to our car and proceed straight down that street. When we came to the end, we were to turn left and continue. Several blocks further on we would come upon a waiting car which would lead us on to our next destination.

With a big bear hug and a kiss, we left and again stepped out into a beautiful day. With such clear instructions there was no difficulty in proceeding to where another lead car was waiting. I was surprised, though, to see that it was a different car, but I learned later that for safety reasons they had changed vehicles and drivers, and that the driver we were now following was very familiar with the area we were going into.

It was about five o'clock that afternoon when we arrived at our next destination. Going through the same cloak-and-dagger method of getting to the meeting place, we soon found ourselves in a building which had been converted into a large hall. It was jammed with people, and many were standing at the back and down the aisles. I could see who I was speaking to this time, for the bright afternoon sun lit the building very well. I was not surprised to see hungry faces of all ages, eager and receptive to the Word of God. But again there was that startling lack of Bibles! Among several hundred people there was only one or possibly two Bibles.

I had been asked to make my message here brief, for there would be another service in the same place at eight o'clock that evening, and just before I was through preaching a young man jumped up on the platform and began taking pictures with a small camera. Almost before anyone could respond or move, he snapped several shots of the crowd and then disappeared among the throng. The crowd began to disperse, and I noticed that most people held their heads low, even to the point of covering their faces with their hands. After everyone left and only the pastor and I remained in the building, I asked him what had happened and why the reaction. "You're attracting large crowds," he told me, "and word has gone through to the government officials, who want to know the people attending these meetings. Somehow or other this young man managed to get into the meeting with his camera and has attempted to photograph the people. You will note, though, that he didn't have much success, for they were quick in responding and covering their faces."

When I heard this, and remembering the eight o'clock service scheduled there that evening, I was sure that no one would be in attendance. But my presumptions were wrong, and the hall was jammed with people again. I can honestly say that this was one of the greatest services we ever had.

There was no place for us to stay in this town that night, so after the meeting we were joined by another believer, who rode with us and led us to another small town about thirty kilometers away. Here we were taken to a house which was also used as a meeting place for believers. It was far after midnight when they brought me to an upstairs room which was to be my bedroom. It was very small, allowing just enough space for a single bed and a small nightstand. But after such a busy day, I found this room a most welcome sight!

I was alone again, an occasion that was most infrequent as we traveled among our Iron Curtain believers. Weary as I was, I wanted to use some of these precious moments to commune with God, so I knelt at my bedside and began to pray. In the quietness of that midnight hour I heard a faint voice. Listening carefully, it seemed to be coming from under the bed I was about to retire into. When the voice came again I crawled under the bed, but there was not a sound in that room! Rather perplexed, I fell into bed and because of my weariness, quickly went off to sleep.

I had forgotten all about the mysterious voice the next morning when I joined the pastor again. This day was spent making contact with several believers in the area. Before leaving Canada, God had provided us with a substantial amount of money for assistance to persecuted Christians. Today I was to see some of these people firsthand and to witness their needs.

The church I was in was an unregistered one. I will take a moment to explain the difference between a registered church and an unregistered one. In most Iron Curtain countries the government maintains strict control of all religious organizations. To be recognized by the government, the church body has to sign a document letting the government run their affairs and has to agree to several conditions, such as not baptizing anyone under eighteen years, refraining from an altar call or persuading anyone to accept Jesus Christ, avoiding teaching religious beliefs to children, and eliminating any outreach beyond the existing congregation. Those refusing to sign a document to this effect are not recognized by the government and are thus an "unregistered" or "underground" church. These churches are constantly under surveillance from government officials and secret police and are subject to severe persecution.

At almost midnight we said good-bye to the last believer, and as the pastor and I went upstairs I remembered the voices I had heard each night as I went to sleep. When I asked him about it he smiled and said, "Tomorrow you'll find out. Just go to bed now and have a good rest." That was all the coaxing I needed, and, although the occasional sound of a voice crept into the room, I fell sound asleep.

Early the next morning a loud knocking came on my door. Jumping out of bed I met the pastor, who said, "Hurry, let's go!" Without further question I dressed quickly and went out with him.

Leaving the building, we proceeded around the outside corner and, about halfway around, came to a set of stairs leading to lower quarters within the same structure. There were fourteen steps leading down, and it appeared that they were not in use because of their run down condition. Leaning against the wall over the stairs were several old broken window frames which we squeezed past to descend the steps.

At the bottom was a door which the pastor unlocked, leading into a room about twelve by thirty feet. Inside I saw eighty men and women on their knees on the dirt floor, praying and weeping before God for revival in their country. Hearing us come in, they all sat up on the small wooden benches around the room, and, wiping their eyes, began looking at us. I have never seen such a sight in my life, and all at once it dawned on me . . . this was where the voices were coming from that I had been hearing in my room! When these people completed their work shift, instead of going home they would secretly come to this lower room where they could pray and ask God for revival!

The presence of God was so real in that room that preaching came easy, and for the next hour-and-a-half I shared with these people. As I preached they began weeping again and continued weeping throughout my message. It was an experience I shall never forget. When I was through, everyone knelt down and began praying again.

The pastor looked at me for a moment as he noted the look of amazement on my face, and then he explained, "These people have been praying here in this room all their spare hours for the last twenty days. They are convinced that this is the only key to revival for our land. And, like these ones here, there are hundreds of other groups across the whole country who are praying the same way." "You see," he continued, "in your country you can pray like this openly, but here we cannot."

Tears filled my eyes and my heart ached as I left that room while those faithful saints continued to beseech God for revival. "Surely God will use everything we have to share for faithful servants like this," I thought.

The service had begun at seven in the morning, and upon leaving we were whisked across the countryside to another relatively small church where hundreds of people were packed into its small sanctuary. When they saw me arriving they began weeping, for they had been waiting for some time and found it almost impossible to believe that they would be having someone from another country coming to share Jesus Christ with them. The presence of the Lord was so great that I found it easy to preach, and, although I spoke for only twenty minutes, when I asked if there was anyone who would like to surrender his heart to the Lord, about sixty souls came forward and accepted Christ that day. It was easy to see that these people meant business for Jesus as they wept before God, pouring their hearts out to him at the roughly made altar. It was so crowded that there was hardly any place to move, but I knew that God was doing a work in these hearts, for they realized that as they made this decision for Jesus Christ they were rejecting the state and would now become the object of cruelty and persecution from it. They also knew that now as they served Jesus they would lose whatever few liberties and freedom they had and would move into the ranks of a third- or fourth-class citizen facing the threat of imprisonment at the drop of a hat. But it was easy to see that they also knew they had come to the living

Jesus, who promised that in spite of trials and persecutions, He "had come that they might have life, and that they might have it more abundantly" (John 10:10b).

Chapter 5

The Need

My God shall supply all your need according to his riches in glory by Christ Jesus.

—Philippians 4:19

My first trip behind the Iron Curtain did much to make me realize the multitudes of needs among these persecuted Christians, and how unaware we are of the great freedom and liberty we have back in our free countries.

As I mentioned earlier I was appalled at the lack of Bibles, hymnbooks, and Christian literature. Hundreds of times the cry echoed from lips of pleading countrymen, "Help us get Bibles and hymnbooks!" In one place there was only one Bible for a whole congregation of several hundred people. This precious Book was not like the Bibles we are used to having. Every letter and word in it had been copied by hand. I could see the hundreds and hundreds of hours that had been spent so that a congregation could have one Bible! The pages of neatly written words were now showing evidence of wear, and it was clear to see that hungry hearts had handled it many times.

"What can we do, if only temporary, to help relieve this situation?" I asked myself. "After all, if people are so hungry for God's Word that they are willing to spend weeks and weeks to copy it by hand, surely there must be something we can do to help!" I thought. Then the idea hit me! What if we were to provide some type of copying equipment so that they could reproduce what they print by hand? Sure, it wouldn't be like a real printing press, but even the roughest copy of Christian literature is more than appreciated in the countries where there isn't any otherwise. "If we can only get a Gestetner duplicator," I planned, "then they, with a typewriter, can increase their production of Christian literature a hundredfold." But the next question was, "How do we get a typewriter, and especially a duplicator? State authorities will surely want to know the reason a Gestetner duplicator is being brought into the country, and when they find out they will surely block it."

I began praying about this, for surely there had to be some way. It seemed as if God was speaking to me, and a voice told me to dismantle the Gestetner and have it brought in piece by piece! This way, pieces of the treasured unit could be slipped into the bottoms of suitcases and briefcases and even into overcoat pockets, and then brought across the borders.

Our plan was put to work. Great prayer went up to God as several people, each from a different profession and with a different purpose, converged on different border points. The prayer was that God would allow these men to enter, each with the precious Gestetner part undetected. No man was instructed to lie, for we all agreed that in God's business it is not necessary to break His own laws. Gradually, piece by piece, the Gestetner began arriving. From one area would come a roller, while another direction brought the crank. Gears arrived in envelopes while other intricate pieces were dug out of deep pockets. Soon a printing machine was being assembled, and as each piece came there was more testimony of the power of our living God! One told of how in great prayer he came upon the border crossing. He was confident that God would have to perform a miracle, for his mission was to bring one of the larger pieces, which could not be concealed in a suitcase. Instead, he had laid it on the front seat of his car with a couple of other items sitting on top of it. Guards converged on the car in front and stripped it from one end to the other. As he waited his turn there was nothing he could do but pray. There was no doubt that today was going to be a real test of God's protection and divine intervention.

"Show me a miracle!" he pleaded with God as time ticked on and they searched the other car. "Only Jesus can help me now," he thought, looking at the important Gestetner part lying so very obviously on his front seat. There was no way now that he could make an attempt to cover it or even to turn back. Finally the other car was moved and the guards were signaling him to move forward. As they did, an official inside called to several of them, leaving just one at the inspection post. His heart leaped in excitement, for now there was only one person to face, and as he moved forward the guard stuck his head inside the driver's window inquiring if he had anything. "Just what is in the front seat," he replied, motioning to the other seat. At that the guard stepped back and motioned him on. God had done it again, and another crucial part was on its way to becoming part of a Christian printing machine!

It wasn't long before our first effort was a reality, for God had blessed our plans by allowing every single piece of the Gestetner to arrive inside the Iron Curtain without being confiscated or even questioned! Now came the intricate job of assembling this unit as plans were made to bring in a typewriter to hasten the copying process.

It wasn't hard to locate the typewriter with the proper characters and letters for this country, but then came the question of how to get the machine across the border without creating suspicion. "If we were to have a portable typewriter packed among a businessman's belongings as he crossed into the country for a few days, chances are they would never even question it," I thought, so I proceeded in getting that kind of typewriter. Hearing of our efforts and plans, many people were willing to bring it along with their luggage, so I prayerfully selected one whom I chose to do the job. It worked just as we planned, and the typewriter was in the hands of those who needed it within a matter of days.

Hundreds of pages of blank paper crossed the borders in briefcases within the next several weeks, and as men within worked around the clock to type needed songbook pages and portions from the Bible, materials were arriving so that they could start production. Finally the day arrived when everything was there and they were ready to go. Carefully they placed the first page on the Gestetner, set up the ink, and started turning the handle. Eager hands fondled that first copy and a shout of praise went up to God! Soon these pages were being folded and sewn by hand into books that would be cherished and used by hundreds of people. In hymnbooks alone, five hundred were produced from the supplies we had given these believers.

Chapter 6

The Word Goes In

Distributing to the necessity of saints....
— Romans 12:13

A most touching incident happened to me during one of my meetings. A young girl about fifteen began to edge her way to the front of the church. She was having the most difficult time because of the crowd and caught my attention in her attempts. Thinking that perhaps she wanted to talk to me, I watched her as she came forward, but she came only as far as a little table which had been used as the pulpit. On it was a small green Bible which one of the ministers had left there during the altar service. For several moments she just stared at the Book, then finally she reached down and picked it up. Her face lit up with joy as she opened the Bible and began reading from its pages. She then closed it and embraced it, then began reading again. She did this several times, and each time tears coursed down her cheeks.

Moving near the girl, I asked her if she would like to own a Bible like the one she was reading. There was a tremendous radiance on her face as she expressed that she would. I promised her that I would get her one, and as I did she began hugging the Bible she was holding in her hands, and, turning to her friends, she said, "That preacher has promised to get me a green Bible just like this one."

Word traveled fast, and in just moments I was thronged with young people asking me to get them a Bible. Seeing their desire, I promised each one I would get them a Bible, but to my great sorrow I was only able to bring them a total of twelve Bibles, which meant that several of these precious young people had to go away without a Bible. This moved me in an even greater way to become involved in this work full-time.

We were always excited when we received a shipment of Bibles from Canada, and even though I had made my headquarters in an area where there was freedom to receive this precious cargo, I now had the task of seeing it arrive safely in the Iron Curtain countries.

One day we carefully packed two hundred Bibles in the trunk of our car. Prayerfully we laid out plans of entering the country, selecting a new entry point to create as little suspicion as possible. As much as possible we would rotate our ports of entry, as this way there would be less chances of guards recognizing us.

As we proceeded toward the border, even though we were still a great distance from it, a good feeling swept over my soul. I felt confident that everything was going to be all right and that we would be able to bring our precious cargo into the country. Nearing the border point, I saw a large sign which read, "You are entering into forbidden area. Chuck all your documents before entering." Upon seeing this my faith left me, and I felt completely alone, forgetting that I still had a heavenly Father who was watching over me.

As we came within sight of the border, I remembered that we could still pray, and pray I did! Again God confirmed that He would get us through. A burly border guard inspected our passports and then asked me to open the trunk of the car. Again, my hope dropped as I fumbled with the keys. "What would I tell this man when he saw the four boxes of Bibles?" There was a long pause after the trunk was opened. He looked at the boxes neatly packed on the floor, then he turned and stared at me. It seemed like an eternity when he removed his eyes from me and focused them on the boxes of Bibles again. Not a single word was said—only stony silence. Then he turned to me and said harshly, "Close the trunk."

I was quick in responding to his order, and with a quick lift of the hand he waved us through. We were now on our way into the country with our load of Bibles. Our destination was some 135 kilometers from the border, and we lost no time in getting there. The pastor met us and welcomed us to his home, where we waited for darkness to set in, for we knew that if we were seen removing boxes from the back of our car, suspicions would be aroused.

When it came time to unload, we carefully laid our clothes over the boxes, and as we entered the house it looked as if we were carrying our clothing in for the evening. One by one Christians from different parts of the area arrived. Without much formality the pastor saw that each person received one or two Bibles. All through the night this went on, and by morning the two hundred Bibles had been distributed, evenly going to different areas so that more people could read and hear the living Word of God. I could see that a chain had been set up to effectively spread the Word around.

There was no way that the pastor would consider allowing us to return from their place that evening. Considerable time had been consumed distributing the Bibles we brought, and it was far past midnight when all was completed.

I am sure God wanted us to stay and see what was happening, for as the Bibles were given out our hearts were touched at the hunger we saw on the faces of these people as they received them. This wasn't a hunger for food, but for the Word of Life. Tears of joy were shed as they handled the Book so precious to them, many of them even kissing and fondling it to make sure that they had actually received a Bible.

One man took several Bibles with him. Realizing the scarceness of these Bibles coupled with the great demand, I began to inquire why they were allowing him the extra copies while they allowed others only one or at the most two. They explained that he had volunteered to go several kilometers further inland to bring these to separate churches. There would be one Bible per congregation, which was something these congregations never had before. And he would undertake the whole trip by foot, traveling under cover of darkness with his precious briefcase of Bibles.

We went to bed that night thanking God for being a part of His work here, and after a short rest we left early the next morning. About twenty kilometers out we were stopped by a policeman. He searched our car, for information had somehow reached the police that Bibles were being transported into the country. Naturally a car with a foreign license plate would be suspected, and we became prime targets. Going through the trunk, under the seats, and inside the doors, the policeman couldn't find anything. He made us open our suitcases and remove the contents, but to no avail. Then he asked us for our papers, and after thoroughly checking them he handed them back then turned and left.

We began rejoicing in the Lord as we repacked our suitcases and reassembled our car, for we were both thinking of yesterday as we drove into this country. At almost this same spot a police car had been parked, and the police were checking another vehicle as we were coming in with our cargo of Bibles. Perhaps it was because the police were so involved with that car that they failed to see us or stop us. But I would rather believe that it was the protecting hand of God who was taking care of us, for just before we left we had prayed and asked not only for His guidance but also His protection. After all, His word says, "The angel of the Lord encampeth round about them that fear him, and delivereth them" (Psalm 34:7).

Chapter 7

A Monumental Task

With God all things are possible.
—Matthew 19:26

As my travels behind the Iron Curtain continued, I not only realized the need for Christian literature there, but also other ways that we in the free world could help. I met with families who would tearfully tell how their relatives and forefathers had to flee from Russia to China in the early thirties, where they lived until China fell under Communism in the late forties. Now these same people were being harassed by Chinese Communists and were being forced back into Russia.

I had seen letters about great persecutions of Christians in China, especially foreign Christians, and these letters were confirmed when the Reverend Claire Scratch, a missionary in China, was released from prison there and returned to Canada with the same news. Folks were unable to find work, and those who did were now being squeezed from their jobs. In great groups they were moving from place to place, praying and searching for a way to enter a free country.

Upon hearing about this I contacted the Red Cross, who told me the only thing that could be done now was to send them food and clothing. We had names of hundreds of families, and through the Red Cross we made initial contact and began sending them food and clothing parcels.

The cry of these people was to be set free, but we could not find a free country that would accept them. Pressure was being put on them to return to their homeland, but they knew that there they would now face even more persecution. We could not allow this to happen, but what could we do?

Realizing that we had done all that man could do, we began seeking God for an answer. After a siege of fasting and prayer, it seemed that God was directing me to Canadian immigration authorities. This seemed an impossible situation, for on many previous occasions I had gone to them only to learn that Canada was closed to these people.

But still that urge continued, and I'm sure the bleak winter weather reflected my feelings as I approached the authorities again. I must admit I almost felt a spirit of defeat, but still something inside urged me on.

By this time I suppose I had become a familiar face in that office, and sometimes I felt that as they saw me coming they would find something to busy themselves so that they would not have to face my persuasive questions about getting the people over. Today, however, there was a different atmosphere as I was ushered into the office. "I believe I have good news for you," the official exclaimed as he pointed to a seat. "Although Canada is still under the same restrictions and rulings as before, we understand that now Paraguay and Australia have opened their doors for displaced persons from within the Bamboo Curtain. From what information we can get, a sponsor is required and there are considerable details to be worked out, but if you would like, I am sure we could put you in touch with the proper authorities to get the ball rolling." It seemed like I was in a dream, and I nervously fumbled with my hands as the official scratched the name and address of both consulates in Canada.

It wasn't long before I was in their offices, and, though details were in some aspects different, the general plan was the same. "Yes, we could now sponsor people out of Bamboo Curtain countries. It had to be on the desire or wishes of the parties involved, and the sponsor would have to assume financial responsibility." This was music to my ears, but what was this financial responsibility the sponsor would have to assume?

Soon it was all spelled out to me. Countries welcoming these people could not assume responsibility for their fares or other transportation costs. That didn't seem too bad, for it would be easy to raise private money for their fares. But then came the big blow! If we were willing to sponsor a person into the country, we would have to guarantee forty dollars a month for that person for up to five years if that person couldn't get a job. This took care of them until they were established and relieved the government of the financial burden. Forty dollars per month, 480 dollars per year, 2400 dollars per five years, plus travel fare, for every person we brought over! Would we be able to meet these requirements?

As I pondered over the red tape set before me

I began to think of the requests I had received. They included everything from a single individual to a family of several. This meant that God would have to provide a great amount of money if we were to get these people released. But there was hope, for if we could get them into either Paraguay or Australia they could find jobs and start supporting themselves as well as save up money to proceed to Canada or the United States, for from Paraguay or Australia they could freely make their way onward.

As I continued traveling I was able to share this need with many churches. When believers in the free world heard the despairing stories of less fortunate brethren, great sacrifices were made to raise the necessary funds. Widows came forth with the widow's mite and pensioners brought in what was probably their total savings. Small children brought donations, evidence of emptied piggy banks and other caches of savings. All was freely and cheerfully given and God was bound to bless it, for the Word says, "God loveth a cheerful giver" (2 Corinthians 9:7).

As Bibles, Christian literature, hymnbooks, and financial assistance continued seeping through the Iron Curtain to believers within, work was progressing greatly in another part of the world, where newfound hope was being experienced by Christians as they found that means were being prepared to afford them freedom.

It was a monumental task, requiring much prayer and the wisdom of Solomon. There was no way we could separate a family, so if we had a request to bring seven members we had to consider them all and raise 16,800 dollars to cover the guarantee we made to the government before we could bring them out. Then there was the task of raising the fare for each of them as well as whatever other costs were involved. Needless to say, it was never easy to work with Bamboo Curtain officials to make final arrangements.

I remember one family we were able to free from the bondage of Communism. God had spoken to them many years before, and they had started their long trek to freedom. He had told them He would lead them across Russia, through China, and to Shanghai. Then He would bring them into the free world. Many hardships were experienced by this family before they got to freedom. Housed in a small commune, they were given rations of food which were at first adequate but were later decreased to starvation level. But God still had a way of caring for this family, and one evening one of the family members came home with an armful of carrots, squash, and other foods. Where had this young person obtained this food in such supply? Mother soon learned that the children had noticed in passing the Chinese graveyard that people offered food to their deceased loved ones to help them in the other world. As the children watched from their hiding places, they realized that this was a way God was providing for them, so they helped themselves to the food after the mourners were gone. This worked for a while, until authorities caught up with them. Then they were forbidden to take that food again, and as it rotted in the cemetery less rations were forthcoming.

More Russian families were arriving and food

was getting scarcer. Living quarters were limited and very rugged. People were having to sleep on the dirt floor as one family shared with another, and when the government found out about the sharing, all food supplies were cut off to them. This particular family was one of them, and as they looked to the bare closet for food, they saw only enough rice and dried fish for several meals for this family alone, never mind the added family that had joined them. The mother prayed and brought the need before God. For the next several days this family witnessed a miracle, for the food met their need and continued to be available from the almost-empty containers days after they should have been empty.

This family also related an incident in which the children came home sobbing hysterically. In passing the graveyard a stench filled their nostrils that was so vile it was impossible to describe. Just outside the wall of the cemetery they saw a large bonfire. Investigating further, they heard piercing screams break through the afternoon, and to their horror they saw Chinese people being burned alive. A few days later they discovered that these were Chinese Christians that the soldiers had burned at the cemetery.

This family made continuous contact with government officials but were told they would never get to America. But they could not realize that God had His hand in this and was about to fulfill His promise made to them several years before. In spite of all resistance and opposition from government authorities, we were responsible in getting the release of this family and locating them in Australia.

As the years went by, they were able to provide for themselves and save enough money to bring them to the beloved country God had called them to, America!

It is easy now to see the reason why, for these people have been a tremendous testimony of the saving and keeping power of the Living God. And over the years a member of this family has shared testimony in churches across America and Canada, challenging people with the need behind the Curtained countries.

Also, as she experienced the new freedom God gave her, she fully realized the Christians' responsibility to their brethren behind the Iron and Bamboo Curtains. Seeing the effectiveness of World Christian Ministries to these people, she made her way to one of our offices, where she shared the burden with us that she wanted to become part of this organization.

Living in America and Canada and sharing her testimony of the need and of God's provision might have been accepted by some as a means of helping out, but she wanted to do even more! Her conviction was so great that she volunteered the assistance of herself and her husband.

For several years they visited churches on this side of the ocean. But as soon as they raised enough money they took the great risk of returning to the country where she was born and rejected, so that beloved brothers and sisters in the Lord could receive encouragement from the Word of God.

As I think of this family, I realize it is but one of several hundred that came to freedom in that time of great need. Each one has a different story to tell, but from them all came confirmation of the greatest need, and that is for Bibles. I am challenged to think that as we live without fear here and can freely read the Word of God and share it with others, there are so many thousands and thousands of people who want the Bible but can't even get a copy of it.

Some people who visit the Iron Curtain countries come back with word that Bibles are freely on sale in stores in cities they have visited. I have seen these stores and visited them myself, only to find that they are nothing but a propaganda front for tourists to see, and that if we move to the inward parts of the countries where tourists don't go, we find that there are no Bible stores whatsoever, and that when government authorities find out a person has a Bible, the Book is seized and destroyed!

Instead of getting less the demand is getting greater, for in Russia alone the underground church is estimated at over ten million born-again believers. In spite of severe persecution, loss of jobs, and a multiplication of hardships, believers are increasing and so is the need for the Word of God.

Chapter 8

Reaping

The harvest truly is plenteous. . . .
—Matthew 9:37

As a Bible courier behind the Iron Curtain, on nine different occasions I traveled alone on these missions. After I became familiar with the countries and their customs and reactions, I found it much easier to travel alone. Naturally a person is less suspected if he travels alone, and brethren within the country have more confidence when they have only one person to deal with. Needless to say, these brethren are key people in the work, for they are able to direct where to go and they assist in many matters, such as arranging contacts and places to stay, showing where the need is the greatest, setting up meetings, and above all, providing identification, which is necessary among the cautious people.

Whenever I go into a country with Bibles, literature, song books, or money, I am always asked to speak to the underground church and give them words of encouragement. As you will note from previous chapters, it is never difficult to get great crowds in spite of all the dangers involved.

A great number of people had turned out for an afternoon meeting we were holding. The cold

January weather might have discouraged them, but still they were there. The only heat in the place came from those attending, and, though wraps and heavy coats were evident, there was a warmth in that place that only God could give.

After I finished speaking I overheard some of the brethren speaking behind me. Although I couldn't understand what they were saying, I knew they were talking about me, for I would hear "Derkatch" this and "Derkatch" that. Becoming a little concerned, I asked my interpreter what they were talking about. He told me that it really didn't concern me, and he suggested that he take me home. Forgetting the incident, I went on to the place at which I was staying and enjoyed the fellowship of my host and hostess as we partook of a hearty meal.

It was just dusk and I had hardly finished eating when an old Volkswagen drove up to the house. Arriving inside was my interpreter, who said, "Let's go." I asked him where we were going, and he said to another service. Satisfied, I settled back into the seat to pray as we moved forward.

All of a sudden a motorcycle appeared in front of us and another appeared in back. There were two heavily bundled men on each one, and as we traveled over the rough road they continued to escort us. The trip was about 35 kilometers, and as we arrived darkness had set in and I was not sure where we were, although I knew it was a small village. When the car stopped I noticed several men coming toward us, and without a word they picked up the car with ourselves inside, carried it over a ditch, and pushed it through a muddy yard into a barn.

Quickly the door was closed, and through the two dim kerosene lamps I could see that the building was jammed with people. They immediately ushered me to a table, and as they did the crowd began singing. Sitting in the semidarkness, I detected that only about eight people out of the crowd of over three hundred were singing. Several songs were sung and then one of the brothers prayed. Following the prayer, another brother turned to me and said, "Preach."

Each exercise of the service seemed to be done in almost a military fashion, and as I began speaking I became very aware that this group of people was not acquainted with what I was saying. As I shared the gospel with them many showed great interest, and tears were in the eyes of many. Explaining how Jesus Christ had died on the Cross for their sins and wanted to become their Savior now, I concluded my talk with an invitation for them to accept Christ into their hearts. Several indicated their desire to follow Christ, and we prayed for them. Immediately after that prayer I was asked to leave and go to the waiting car, which I did, leaving the crowd behind. As the car was backed out, several men picked it up again after pushing it through the mud, lifted it over the ditch and onto the road, and we started for home.

I was rather bewildered about this service, especially the extreme secrecy and military fashion in which it was carried out. Through the darkness I could see our two motorcycle escorts, but the one behind now only had one person on it instead of the two that were on it before. I asked the interpreter what happened to the other man that was on the motorcycle when we went to the service. "Now that it's all over, I'll tell you the whole story," he replied.

"The man left behind is pastor of the new work where we have been tonight. When he heard you were in the area, he asked for permission to have you preach there, but the government authorities refused him permission.

"He has been working diligently to get a work going, but resistance has been extreme from the police. In order to hold a service, he would meet in a basement, crawling through a window to get there. The police knew his intentions and would watch for him on the streets, so he had to do it this way in order to avoid being detained by them. When the service was over he would crawl back through the window and make his way home.

"Authorities would only grant him permission to hold services if he had fifteen believers, and they knew he had only seven. They were making an all-out effort to hamper him in any way from obtaining more believers, for they knew if he obtained fifteen he could then request a legal permit to assemble together.

"Knowing this need, we were persuaded to bring you to this service. By not telling you what was happening, you could honestly be ignorant of the details if police were to find out. This way you would not lie, and he would take all the blame, leaving you to go free from any punishment. Although we were free from police intervention tonight, there may be an investigation in the morning which can still possibly mean jail for him. If no one reports the meeting, we have made plans for him to join us tomorrow morning at eleven."

I didn't sleep much that night, wondering if a person who went to such a great risk as he had would remain undetected by the authorities. I was amazed at his plan he had carried out which absolved me of all blame, and as I tossed in my bed I prayed for his protection.

The next morning I awaited the eleven o'clock train which would bring him to us if he hadn't been reported. Anxiously my eyes scanned the people as they disembarked from the train. Among them I spotted the pastor, and as he came toward me I could still see the mud on his feet from the muddy yard we had been in the night before.

There was a smile on his face and great rejoicing as we greeted each other. Then he filled us in on the details. "Last night when you all left the meeting, there were many interested in finding Christ," he said. "I had the privilege of leading eight men to Christ," he continued, and many others were praying too! God really placed His seal of approval on the meeting, and now we have fifteen or more Christians in that village and will be able to go ahead for Christ."

"What about reaction from the police or other officials about the large gathering?" I inquired.

"God was in that too!"

"How?" I continued.

"He must have blinded their eyes. Also, those I selected to attend, even though they were not

Christians, did not elect to report it, for this morning I waited until the train came by, and had anyone reported it they would have arrested me by then. When nothing happened, I caught the train and came to this meeting." As I looked at this excited preacher with his tattered clothes and mud-covered shoes I thought of what Paul said to the Romans in Chapter 10, verse 15: "How beautiful are the feet of them that preach the gospel of peace and bring glad tidings of good things!"

Traveling among the Christians is not an easy task, for their needs are so heartbreaking. God had given us several wonderful meetings in one place, and a middle-aged lady came into one of the services from a long distance away—I believe she said it was seven hundred kilometers. She pleaded with the local minister to go to her village and hold meetings, stating that she had been sent by the brethren to make this request. In despair they had to tell her there was no one available.

"Why can't the Canadian come?" she inquired, not wanting to give up. The time on my passport had just about expired, so I tried to explain to the lady that I couldn't go either. Tearfully she pleaded, but there was nothing I could do either—that is, until an idea struck me: could they possibly use a gospel service on tape? That would be fine, but where would they get tape recorders? I assured them I would make arrangements so that they could have a recorder to record the services, and then the minister in the other village would have one to play the services back on. All of a sudden, as this woman realized what was happening, a great joy swept her face. Now they would be able to share in the great gospel service which this larger church was having.

Now I realized why God allowed me to have extra local currency in my possession, for before I left the country I was able to purchase two tape recorders, items which were totally out of reach of any struggling church budget within that country. God had even made it possible to obtain an ample supply of tapes so that services could be taped every week and sent on to the village area.

Some time later I noticed a letter in the mail postmarked from that village. Excitedly I opened the travel-worn letter, and with just a bit of thinking and reading between the lines I was able to decipher the message. It read, "We are very pleased at the working of the new instrument we now have. It is put to a great use and many can now enjoy it.

"We know that over two hundred in the last month were able to decide they liked it. Many more are considering and we ask you to remember them."

The message was clear! They had received the tape recorder and it was being well used. Over two hundred had accepted Christ through it, and many more were considering. I thought of another passage in Romans. "How then shall they call on him in whom they have not believed? And how shall they believe in him of whom they have not heard? And how shall they hear without a preacher?" God provided the preacher through the tape recorder!

Chapter 9

Hunger

I was hungry, and you gave me food.
Matthew 25:35

It was hard to believe, as I traveled within these countries, that the war had been over for several years. Christians were having cloak-and-dagger experiences in order to worship the Savior they loved so much. Hovering over them all the time was the fear of being reported to authorities—and retaliation.

A faint glimmer of hope had risen during the war years, for the countries had called upon the Christians for their assistance in the war effort. The authorities knew that Christians were honest and conscientious and made good workers in the war and munition plants. So pressures were taken off from them as they came to the aid of their country. But now the war was over, and with each year came increasing pressures on them.

How can we understand what it's like to go to church where there's not even a Bible? The minister has to preach from parts of the Scripture committed to memory, or perhaps someone has a single page or two from one of the Gospels. Until you actually see it, there is great difficulty in picturing this situation in your mind. I had seen it so often, but again it was brought out so clearly to me on one particular trip.

I had been in a service which lasted well after midnight. Being weary from traveling, I was anxious to find a place of rest for a couple of hours, and I felt that it would be all I could do to get there. Settling in my mind that this would be my next step, I relaxed a minute in my chair when a brother leaned over and said, "Don't go home yet; we want you to come to our prayer meeting." "Why in the world would they be holding a prayer meeting at this hour?" I thought. "Can't they find a more earthly hour to do it in? There go those few precious minutes of rest I had planned." But as I grumbled to myself a small voice inside me urged me to go cheerfully.

When the lights were turned out and the folks had made their way toward home, we went out into the darkness of night and on into the countryside. A new moon was counteracting the darkness with its white light, and through the shadows I could see a silhouette of a large barn that we were approaching. As we neared, a murmur could be heard from the inside, penetrating the otherwise still and silent night.

Inside there were scores of young people on their knees on the cold dirt floors, praying and seeking the face of God. For three hours or more they continued without stopping, praying for a revival in that community. My heart wept with them as they continued to look toward the Lord, and the weariness in my bones left as I felt ashamed of myself for being so selfish and wanting that rest in the first place.

It was only days later that word reached me from that community. Revival had broken out! Saints with Holy Ghost boldness like Peter in the Book of Acts had dismissed all fear of retaliation and began witnessing to friends and relatives. Many were surrendering to Christ, and the prayers of these young people were being answered! There are times when man can make barriers to stop his fellowman, but it is impossible to make an Iron Curtain big enough or tall enough to stop the moving of the Spirit of our living God!

In the larger cities it is often more difficult for the Christian to have worship and fellowship because of the danger of neighbors or even relatives turning them in to the police. I learned that much more caution was needed as I contacted believers in these places, especially if I was asked to minister to them.

How does a stranger in a city make necessary contact with the right person and go from place to place without being detected? Many methods are used, but the one I liked the most was shown me by believers within.

As soon as initial contact was made (usually arranged through others I had contacted in neighboring towns or communities), direction was given to a certain hotel. This became my place of residence and central point of all activities. The contact would instruct me that on, say, six o'clock that night I was to leave the hotel and travel in a certain direction for so many blocks. As I neared that point a man stepped out in front of me, and I followed him until he turned off. Across the street was another man continuing in this direction, and when I saw him make a turn I was to turn the other direction and continue for a certain number of blocks, where another man stepped in front of me. Following him, I was instructed to take a certain door on a certain side after a specific number of blocks. Although he continued walking as I approached the door, someone would be there to let me in and direct me to wherever the meeting was located. To return to my hotel, similar instructions were given, and in the darkness of night in a strange city I proceeded as if I had been there all my life!

On one occasion like this I was led into a secret meeting of ministers. There were a total of fifteen present, and I was asked to expound the Word to them. As I started to minister I was shocked at the sight I saw. For fifteen ministers there were only eight Bibles! My first thought was, "Weren't they interested enough to bring along their Bibles?" But then I realized that they didn't even *own* a Bible! What a shame! Here were men who were risking their lives and futures for God, and yet they didn't even have His textbook in their possession!

There is such a great need that one minister who didn't have a Bible came and asked me to persuade one of his fellow ministers to share half his Bible with him. Carefully they took the Book apart so that he could have at least *some* of the Holy Bible in order to be able to preach the Word of God.

In another area, hearing that I had some Bibles, I was approached by an old man and a nine-year-old boy. They both stood side by side begging me for a Bible. Another young man who had received Christ into his heart was given two hours by the authorities to reject Him. Boldly he faced them, telling them he didn't need two hours, for he would never reject Christ who had done so much for him.

Angered by his answers and his bold stand for Jesus, they beat him up and threw him into prison. I went with a family member to visit him, and as he came to us from the cold, dark prison there was a radiant smile on his face. "It may be hard down here," he said, "but it will be easy in heaven!"

One elderly minister approached me in a meeting with tears in his eyes. "For many years I have been able to make lecture outlines for our young ministers," he explained. "They do not have the privilege of attending Bible colleges like you do in Canada, and they can't even get Bibles to study by. But now look at my hands—they are old and shaky, and I can't write so they can read it any longer. If only I had a typewriter, then I could still do these lectures and help our ministers in their great work for God." It was my privilege to supply him with a typewriter and also a hearing aid, and today from his two-room home he is still using that typewriter to write gospel messages and Bible lectures for the younger preachers who need the guidance of seasoned men of God. What might seem so insignificant to us can be of such great importance to believers in these deprived countries!

As you travel deeper into the country there is a much greater need, for these areas are not touched by tourists and thus, as I explained earlier, they have no access to the Word of God. One trip led me deep into one of these areas, and for 21 days I did nothing but preach the Word. During that time I had 84 gospel services, and in some of these services, I had to preach twice. Under pressures like these I became so exhausted that my nerves gave out, and they had to take me to a doctor.

After my thorough examination the doctor said to me, "I have found that you're completely exhausted and run down. It is an absolute necessity that you find a place of quietness and take at least one week of complete rest." With those instructions he gave me medication, and then the brethren secretly took me to another village, feeling sure that no one would bother me there during that week.

I was given a small room and a very comfortable bed. It seemed that I had hardly settled down when someone found out I was there. Two or three brethren came into my room, and soon more followed. "Please tell us more about God," they pleaded; "Please preach to us!"

I tried to explain to them that I was exhausted and that the doctor had advised complete bed rest for one week. But they wouldn't take "No" for an answer, suggesting that I preach to them lying down. Finally I gave in and preached twice in that position, but then my body could stand it no longer, and as Jesus and His disciples had to get away and have rest, I was finding myself being taken out of the country, where I could fly to Vienna and have complete rest.

I'm not too sure that I actually got much rest,

for I couldn't dismiss from my mind the desperate need. Nor was it easy, as I rested in Vienna, to forget the fact that in one church I visited with over four hundred members they had only twelve Bibles!

But perhaps it was God's will that I be laid on my back for these few days, for it was during this time that I was able to compile in my mind what I had experienced and seen.

Questions raced through my mind as to how World Christian Ministries could effectively face and conquer such a task for Jesus Christ. Where could we make most effective use of money entrusted to us for this work?

My contacts inside the Iron Curtain and in bordering countries were enabling me to set up an effective system to bring Bibles, literature, and money within. We now have an efficient communication system, so that we can know the openings and needs and be able to act immediately. "But," I thought as I lay on that bed in Vienna, "Surely there is something more we can do." As I dozed off to sleep the sounds of a distant radio broke the silence. I believe I was too tired at that moment to realize that God was showing me another plan!

Chapter 10

A New Plan

Behold, I will do a new thing; now it shall spring forth.

—Isaiah 43:19

I must have slept for several hours, and when I awoke it took me a few minutes to figure out where I was. I didn't know what had awakened me, but again from the distance came the sound of a radio. "It's quite a thing," I thought, "how the sounds of a radio penetrate the air, for even though I don't have one in my room, I'm able to hear one from another room." Then it struck me—God was getting the message across! Why not use the medium of radio to cross the vast countries enshrouded in the Iron Curtain?

I wasn't tired any longer, and now I just had to get back in the swing of things, so not too many days later I was winging my way home with a new plan in my heart.

Over the next several days I took much time to obtain information and statistics about my plan. I found that in the Soviet Union alone there are more than 250 million people, and 90 percent of them have never heard God's Word. That means that a mass of people larger than the population of the United States has never heard a thing about God and His great love. Another startling revelation that I found out was that in the USSR all radio broadcasting is by shortwave, and over 85 percent of the population has shortwave receivers. This was confirming the plan I was thinking about.

Literally millions could be reached with the gospel through radio broadcasts beamed into their country from stations outside. In checking further, I found that radio station IBRA in Portugal had a 25,000-watt transmitter and was broadcasting the gospel throughout Europe in some 21 languages. God showed me that World Christian Ministries was to go on the air there with a program to the Slavic countries.

Much prayer and thought went into this program and its making, for it could not be just an ordinary one, but one that would stop the listener as he flicked the dial and cause him to stay and listen. People all over the world love music, especially if they can hear it on the radio in their own language, so we decided that we must have music in their language to begin the program. In addition to music, the program had to contain the message of the gospel and words of encouragement, so that people would learn not only the concern and compassion of the free world but also the living message from God. So with excellent music and the Word of God we began on the air.

Soon letters were pouring in from Poland, the Ukraine, White Russia, and many other countries. The comments were most encouraging, and in many of them was the suggestion that we read more from the Bible, for they never had a chance to hear it before. "What a good idea!" I thought; "We'll have a section of Bible reading on every program." As this was implemented further suggestions came in, asking especially that we read the Word of God slowly and clearly. The purpose of this was so that people waiting around the radios with pens and papers could copy down the Word and retain it.

This was not a new idea, as men had been known to spend weeks and months in secret rooms where they would work on the task of copying the Word of God letter by letter and word by word, all by hand, so that others could have it. I remember meeting men who shared with me their precious task of copying the Word, and how they explained that after a short time their backs began to ache and their fingers would start to refuse holding the pen. They told of how, during their strenuous task, there were times when their brain went dull from lack of sleep, yet their hunger for God's Word and intense desire for spiritual food drove them on. As the Book took shape, they told of how they would carefully hide it, praying that it would not be discovered and destroyed.

But through radio no one could ever rob them of the Word, for the master copy was in the hand of our announcer and not fearfully tucked away is some home, where the danger of discovery lurked at all times. There was no limit to the amount of people who could gather around the radios across the countries and listen. Above all, they could copy these precious portions of Holy Scripture.

More letters came, and more confirmation that our plan of broadcasting was in the will of God. Almost every letter we received contained a request for a Bible, and, even though the broadcasts were doing a tremendous work, it was heartbreaking to see so many people still starving spiritually. As we read through the tremendous mail we got from the program, we came across many letters like these:

We await the arrival of Tuesday (broadcast time) as if we were awaiting the arrival of our Lord. If possible, please send me a Bible... (Poland).

We are very grateful to God and to you for your broadcast. If only you could see those souls who with earnestness listen to you and join in singing those beautiful songs. Dear friends, do not let your hearts grow faint, but continue working for the glory of God, and do remember that in His eyes your work is not in vain... (USSR).

With encouragement like these letters, we didn't hesitate for opportunities to get on to other radio stations, and now we are broadcasting the gospel to these hungry people from three different directions.

Every request for a Bible is carefully filled and mailed to that person in his own language. Hundreds of letters return which confirm the arrival of the Bibles and express the recipients' sincere gratitude for them.

Not too long ago I was behind the Iron Curtain again and was able to witness what the radio broadcasts were doing. In the churches it was easy to see that more youth were in attendance and that a great awakening was taking place. The Communists do not fear atomic bombs, since they have more than enough of their own, but they really fear the Living Word, which is filtering through the barriers. "The word of God is not bound" (2 Timothy 2:9).

Chapter 11

What About Freedom?

Blessed are ye when men shall revile you and persecute you. . . .
—Matthew 5:11

The question often arises as to how much religious freedom there is in the Soviet Union. Their propaganda machine would lead us to believe that there is a considerable amount, but this is not true, as I have seen firsthand. In the past short while, many of the Christians have left the legal registered church of the Soviet Union because they cannot faithfully serve God while obeying instructions given to church leaders by the government. To back up my statement, I want you to see some of the excerpts from the "Instructive Letter" to presbyters from the All Union Church Council. These excerpts are taken verbatim.

The senior presbyter must remember and know that the main purpose of the services at the present time is not the attraction of new members.

The responsibility of the senior presbyter is to restrain unhealthy missionary developments.

It is a responsibility of the senior presbyter to carefully guard the acceptance of new members into the church, strictly observing the regulations of a testing period of not less than two to three years, so that the churches may get rid of unhealthy practices of competing for quantity of membership.

The senior presbyter should know and fulfill his responsibilities according to the directives, not departing from its contents, and not be involved in too much preaching.

Fewer sermons or less preaching and less attention to the spiritual necessities, and more attention to the supervision of local presbyters and strict fulfillment of regulations concerning receiving new members into the church. This will make the work of our brotherhood practical. The presbyter must be tactful and attentive to the members, fulfilling the directives of the ECHB (All Union Council) and legislation of the Soviet Union about cults.

Every minister is a servant of only his congregation, and he is not permitted to preach and be active outside his church, observing the same with other preaching members of his congregation.

Ministers must not extend invitations to new people to become members of the church.

Executive organs have the responsibility to keep the order of the church services and not to depart from the directives of ECHB and Soviet legislation on cults.

Believers must definitely get rid of narrow ideas on art, literature, radio, television, etc.

Examination of those willing to become members of the church is to be done by the executive organ.

The baptism of the believers in the age group between 18 and 30 must be brought to a minimum.

Persons baptized by other than the local minister should not be received into membership of the church.

Children of preschool and school age, as a rule, should not be allowed to attend church services. In the past, because of a lack of vigilance on the part of church officials, the following departures from Soviet legislation on cults were noticed:

Baptisms of persons under 18 years of age. Material assistance between members of the church. Bible studies and other illegal gatherings. Recitals, declamations, and reading of religious material.

Excursions and picnics for young people. Bible courses for preachers and choir directors.

Visitations by preachers besides the local preacher to preach in the pulpits, and other infringements of Soviet legislation.

These are not obscure, outdated instructions to the people of the Soviet Union but up-to-date instructions that pastors are expected to abide by. I ask you this question, dear reader: how would you feel worshiping under these conditions? How would you like your pastor to have to work under these conditions? Yet there are many believers who are faithfully sharing God's Word to these people. Continually we are receiving reports from them, some encouraging and others like this one from a hard-working pastor.

"The building was packed to capacity. People were standing four abreast in the aisle, and the overflow filled the courtyard. As the service ended praise began to erupt from those God had blessed. He was there and we all felt His presence.

"After the service several came asking for baptism. They wanted to obey God's Word and follow their Lord in the waters of baptism. To me it was a matter of great concern. No one in Russia made an open confession of Christ and a bold request for public baptism unless he'd had a genuine experience with Christ. I wondered what would happen to the young ones. Would they be expelled from school or their jobs? And the older ones— would their families suffer if they were imprisoned for their commitment to Christ? Our government had a record for brutality, persecution, and imprisonment of those who stood for God. Had the atheistic authorities not claimed total destruction of the Christian faith by 1980?

"The question was perplexing. Should I try to obtain permission for a baptismal service at the river, or should I simply go ahead and do it in secret? I asked God for His will and direction. I felt He wanted me to consult the government authorities.

"I told the officers what I wanted, and at once the opposition began. 'In these modern times no one likes to see people who still cling to old-fashioned ideas of God,' said one. After some discussion another said, 'What harm can it do? People have no interest in religion and baptism. We can simply make his permit for four o'clock in the morning. Who in his right mind would show up at that time?'

"Permission was not only granted but I was promised two Russian soldiers to keep order in case our permission was questioned. This was too good for words. I was overjoyed and quite relieved. We would have our baptismal service, with permission, at 4 A.M. the following week.

"On the appointed morning we got up in darkness and made our way to the river. Already some believers had gathered and had put up the little blanket tents where the candidates for baptism were to change into their robes. After some hymns each one being baptized gave a testimony of what Christ had done in his life. As they went into the water they once again confessed their faith in Jesus Christ as their personal Savior. The waters of the river were cold.

"At about six o'clock a rowboat with three men

aboard put out from shore and came in our direction. They approached where I was baptizing and asked by whose permission I was baptizing these people. I looked toward the shore, hoping to see the two soldiers who were to preserve order in case of trouble. There were none—no one to defend our cause. The three men began to accuse me viciously for having a public show—a stupidity in this land of modern technology. How was it possible that we would even consider baptizing people openly in this way? They grabbed my shirt and pulled me into the boat, repeating their questions about permission and why I was polluting the land with this belief in Jesus Christ. I told them I had a permit from the government and asked what right they had to disrupt the service.

"'I'll show you by what right we are doing this!' shouted one. They rowed the boat into the middle of the river, where they proceeded to beat and kick me. Then they threw me into the river, and two of them jumped in and slapped me and dumped me under the water. I was losing consciousness when they rowed off in their boat.

"I awoke in a hospital some five kilometers from the river. The doctors looked at me and shook their heads. I was covered with black and blue marks and some ribs had been broken. I had lacerations and bruises all over my body. For over a month I was not permitted to see any of the Christians. Then the ban was lifted and some of the believers came to see me. They looked at me and at one another and tears filled their eyes. I assured them I felt better than at any time in my entire Christian walk. (Isn't this what Christianity is all about—serving the King of kings no matter what the cost? Jesus is there to see us through our deepest sorrows, our greatest trials. With Him we are more than conquerors—victors in His name.) The presence of God filled the hospital room and I sensed what God had done in the hearts and lives of those standing around my bed. We rejoiced and praised God. He was real! He was in our land and nothing could keep Him out.

"But, oh, the need for our land—such a desperate need for Bibles, for gospel literature, for radio programs to reach those who have no opportunity to learn of Jesus' saving grace. My heart was breaking for my country. I reached out in prayer to those in the free world who have privileges beyond our comprehension. Oh, that they might be burdened to help us, to pray with us, to unite with us, and to join with us in the mighty harvest that God wants from our land, that Jesus Christ might truly have free reign in the hearts of people across the Communist Bloc, the satellite countries, Red China, and the world. 'And a vision appeared to Paul in the night; there stood a man of Macedonia and prayed him, saying, Come over into Macedonia and help us' (Acts 16:9)."

There were reports like this that challenged me to even greater depths in the work of World Christian Ministries. Loaded with supplies of Bibles and other literature, I was back to Europe again, where I could make more contacts and continue to distribute the precious World of God. As I traveled, more firsthand reports came to me via couriers. One indicated that forty believers were arrested in White Russia within a two-year period for evangelical activity. Sentences of two to five years of hard labor were meted out, and out of the forty arrested five were women. From the Ukraine came word that 65 Christians were imprisoned in one year. Their crime: holding unauthorized prayer meetings.

During a one-year period, reliable sources indicated that in the Soviet Union over one thousand believers were imprisoned for religious crimes, while another report brought the sad news that soldiers opened fire on some four hundred believers gathered for an open air service. Many of them were killed.

God still prodded me on. "There's much more you can do," He said, and shortly I was to find out.

Chapter 12

The Living Power

If any man be in Christ, he is a new creature.

—2 Corinthians 5:17

One day not too long ago a certain religious publication carried an extensive report of one of their leaders who visited the Soviet Union. In this report he spoke of the red-carpet treatment given him while there, and how the Christians were now enjoying religious freedom. He spoke of seeing them worship by the thousands and how Bibles were now available in the bookstores. One thing he did not explain was that this was in the main tourist area of Russia, where the government had made sure that there are showcase churches and that Christians have the Bible available. Their propaganda efforts have proven successful in hoodwinking many visitors to Russia into believing that there is religious freedom there.

A person asked me about this freedom. Having traveled far beyond the reaches of the average tourist, I had to give this honest assessment: "The Christians have the same freedom in the Communist Bloc as a dog on a leash or a bird in a cage. The blood of the martyrs is the seed of the church." To make this statement without backing it up might seem questionable, so I want to share several personal experiences behind the Iron Curtain which show the truth about religious freedom.

In one area I visited and ministered in, a fifteen-year-old girl was saved. Enjoying the joy of finding Jesus Christ as her Savior, she felt that she could go home and share this with her parents, and that they would accept Jesus also. When she got home and told her parents how she was so wonderfully converted in this gospel service, her father, who was one of the leading men in the village, was very provoked about it and replied, "Daughter, you have brought great shame and reproach to our home, and I give you 24 hours of time to reject this Christ, or you must leave home." During the next 24 hours, there was quite a commotion in that home, and, being in a small village, most of the people knew what was going on. The next night, when the time was up, many young people gathered, including a great number of her friends and colleagues as well as some of the town officials, to await outside for her decision. Seeing these people gather, and knowing why they were there, the father brought his daughter out before them and asked her if she had decided to denounce Christ.

As the eager eyes and ears were fixed upon her she replied, "Daddy, how can I reject Christ? How can I denounce God? He has done so much for me; He has saved my life and forgiven my sins, and I know I have a home in heaven. I could never deny Him!" The father then said, "You must go!" and ran back into the house, where he packed her little suitcase with what few clothes she had and an extra pair of shoes.

Opening the door and staring at her, he then said, "Go, and take all these crazy thoughts about God with you!"

Looking at him, she said, "Daddy, could I have one request of you before I leave?"

"Yes, but be in a hurry!"

"Could I pray just before I go?"

"Yes, you may pray on the doorstep."

So on the doorstep, with her suitcase beside her and in front of the many townspeople, she knelt down and began to pray aloud, "Dear heavenly Father, thank You so much for the great plan of salvation, for saving my soul, forgiving my sins, and writing my name in the Lamb's Book of Life, and I know that I have a life hereafter.

"Now, Lord, I have to leave home. I don't know where I am going, but I know that the Spirit of God is going to guide me. I pray, dear Lord, that as I leave this home, please lay this not against my father or mother. Please forgive them, for they know not what they do. I pray also, dear God, that you will save my father, my mother, my brothers and sisters, and my friends here."

Then, picking up her suitcase, she started to walk away when her father tapped her on the shoulder and said, "Daughter, you need not go. While you were praying, the Spirit of the Lord spoke to my heart and I accepted Christ as my own personal Savior. Your mother also accepted Christ during your prayer. You need not go— you're welcome to stay home!"

A wonderful revival then broke out in that area.

This incident had taken place on a Friday night, and on Sunday morning the girl went to church with all her friends. That morning some thirty young people heard the gospel of Jesus Christ for the first time, and every one of them accepted Christ as their own personal savior!

In one of the villages a young boy ten years of age came to a service and listened to the gospel message, and God spoke to his heart. He accepted the Lord Jesus Christ as his own personal Savior. He came from a fairly large family of unsaved people.

When he went home he began telling the family what God had done for him. His parents were very provoked, and even the neighbors were disturbed. They did not know what to do with the little boy— how to persecute him and have him deny the Lord Jesus Christ. They couldn't put him in jail, so they thought of an idea. "If you do not reject Christ," they told him, "You will have to go and live with a family that is very mean, just the husband and the wife with no children, and they are very mean!" This couple was encouraged to be especially cruel to him, and he was to live there until he denied God or rejected the Lord Jesus Christ.

This did not deter his committment to Christ, and when they saw that he wasn't going to back down, they sent him to this place to live. The father thought that surely after one week of misery and not seeing his parents and family he would deny the Lord Jesus Christ and want to return home. But after one week he did not return home, and the parents sent his older brother to persuade him. "Don't you love your mother and father? Don't you love us? Don't you want to come home?" he pleaded. "Sure I do," the ten-year-old replied. "I love my mother and father, brothers and sisters, and my home, but I can't return until you and they accept Jesus Christ. I will not return until then."

"We won't pray!" the older brother told him, "and if you don't quit praying, you'll never be able to come home!"

This continued daily for six weeks—every day his older brother coming to plead with him, "Why don't you come home? Come home and be reunited with your family. We want to see you, we are longing to see you! Your mother and dad want to see you. We want to have you back home." Looking his brother squarely in the eyes, the little boy would ask, "Is my mother praying yet? Is my father praying yet? I love them, but I cannot go home until they pray, until they believe in God."

This continued, and finally the mother said to the father, "There must be something to this. That little boy couldn't be staying with that family for such a long time and under such miserable conditions and being so poorly treated with hardly any food to eat and a cold bed to sleep in, unless there is something to it! I want a Bible; I want to read this Bible and find out what our son has!" Someone was able to find a Bible for her, and she began reading it. God began speaking to her heart, and soon she surrendered her heart to the Lord. Her husband followed, and God moved upon the entire family!

Then the older boy was able to go and assure his little brother, "You can come home now! Your mother is praying, your father is praying, I am praying, we're all praying. Praise the Lord!" The little boy came back home and reunited with his family. There was a great time of rejoicing, and God spoke to so many in that area through this little boy that literally tens and hundreds surrendered to God. This is all because of the faithfulness of a ten-year-old boy and a mother who was honest enough to look for the answer. Thank God there was a person who could give her a Bible where she could find the truth that changed not only her family but the community!

To be a minister of the gospel in the Communist Bloc, you have to be dedicated, brave, and stalwart. I shall never forget the pastor I met during one of my trips inside with Bibles. This was during a large gathering, and a thin, frail man approached me with a very soft, gentle smile and seriously said, "I am enjoying your friendship, your sermons, and your ministry among us. I would like to share a few of my experiences with you, but I cannot do it publicly. Can I talk with you for a little while privately?"

We sought for a place where just the two of us could be, and finally we came to a place within the big hall where we could have that privacy. Then he began to relate his story to me. How thrilling it was to listen to this man of God tell me of the persecution that he endured for the sake of the gospel of the Lord Jesus Christ!

He said to me, "Brother, I was in prison for thirteen years and six months. When I first entered that prison, I was kept in one single cell for eighteen months, and for eighteen months I didn't see a single ray of sunlight or even daylight. I just didn't see anyone except a guard who brought me some food, and every day he asked me to reject the Lord Jesus Christ as my own personal Savior. He said to me, 'Don't you love your family? If you would only reject Christ, you could go home'. The Communists play very heavily on the love of the family or some member of the family. I had to tell that guard that I could not reject the Lord Jesus Christ even though I love my family.

"For eighteen months, Brother, in the dark, damp cell I was miserable, losing many pounds and coming down with a terrible disease. Then they put me in another cell where there was much water, and for six months, day in and day out, there was water dripping on my head constantly. It was so miserable and agonizing that you could almost go insane in that little cell. Every day they would come and ask me to reject Christ as my personal Savior, and every day I would pray and ask God to help me, and, praise God, He did, for never once during those next six months did I think of rejecting the Lord Jesus Christ.

"From there they took me to another cell where there were many other people—in fact, it was so crowded that during the next ten years I was never able to sleep lying down. I could barely sit up because of the crowded conditions. When I entered jail I weighed 193 pounds, but when my release finally came 13½ years later, I hardly weighed one hundred pounds.

"After I was released from jail, the first thing I wanted to see was my wife, my family, and my church. Frail as I was, two men helped me and, assisted by canes, I arrived at my house, where I saw my family.

"I looked at my wife and wept for joy, and so did she. There was a great family reunion, and then I wanted to go and see my church!"

With tears coursing out of his eyes, this brother continued his story to me. "I expected there would be hardly anyone at church after such a long time, but instead I saw many more people there than the day I left. God was good and He had multiplied the church at least three times! My God is good!"

Then, looking me squarely in the eye, he said, "Brother, I have been praying for a Bible for such a long time, and there are just no Bibles available, no gospel literature available whatsoever! My, how I wish I had a Bible!" He looked at my beautiful leatherbound new Bible. He said, "My, I wish I had a Bible like that!" I said to him, "Brother, this is your Bible! You can have it now!" He embraced it, kissed it, and thanked God for that Bible! Thank God I was able to bring that Bible to him! He then told me, "Brother, I have prayed for twenty years for a Bible like this, and today God has answered my prayer!"

Then hear what he had to say as he continued: "During the last few weeks of my imprisonment, a prison guard came over one day with a little revolver and said to me, 'If you do not reject the Lord Jesus Christ as your own personal Savior, I will shoot you. I will kill you!' The power of God fell so mightily upon me that I stood to my feet and looked at him, and he ordered me to back to within five inches of the wall. I obeyed and, looking at him bravely, I told him to shoot me if he wanted to. 'The sooner you shoot me, the sooner I'll be with my Father in heaven.' All of a sudden the man fainted, and within minutes someone came in to remove him from the cell."

The preacher continued his story: "As they left, the power of God left me, and I fell on my face and cried like a little baby, saying, 'Oh God, Oh God! why did that fellow not shoot me? Why did he not kill me? Then I would be relieved of my misery. I want to be with you.' Then tearfully, he added to me, "I was so disappointed and I cried out to God that He would take me home. Then God spoke to my heart and said to me, 'Son, I still have a job for you to do here on earth.' Then I knew I would not be killed and I would not die in prison. Thank God, a few months later I was released, and now you have just given me the tools to preach the Word of God with! I can go out and preach the gospel of Jesus Christ! Brethren, please pray for us! Don't write us off!" For several minutes I just sat there and wept and praised God that He had given us the means to reach into these countries with the Word of God so that these serious needs can be met.

Chapter 13

He Is Able

He shall call upon me, and I will answer him: I will be with him in trouble; I will deliver him and honor him.
—Psalm 91:15

J ust a few weeks ago I received a letter from one of our couriers, who said in his letter that we should pray for a certain family because their three children had been taken away from them. Why? Because the Soviet constitution contains an article about parental rights. These rights are: You should teach and indoctrinate your children in the things of Communism. You must indoctrinate them against God. They must be taught to believe in Lenin and the Communistic teaching.

This mother and father couldn't do it, and instead they were teaching their children the Bible. Because of this the authorities came and took their children away to the state school. The parents will never see them again. This happened in September of 1973.

During the court trial the verdict was that "You are now released of your parental privileges because you did not use them correctly. You have gone against the wishes of the Soviet government." Then the three little children were marched away from the presence of their mother just because she loved God and taught them the Word of God.

The underground church is praying for this family and has requested that we pray for them also, and we certainly will. We thank God for the free countries we live in—the United States, Canada, and the free world. We certainly must help those who are less fortunate than we are here in our free countries.

God works so wonderfully—let me show you how. A few years ago, while I was in the Soviet Bloc, I was in an area where they had allowed us to renovate a building. The brethren told me that if they had eight thousand dollars they could complete the job, and the authorities would grant them permission to do so. World Christian Ministries was instrumental in obtaining the eight thousand dollars for them.

The leading brother said to me, "We want you to be here when we have the opening service." So I made it my business to travel in that area at the time that this church would be opened for gospel meetings.

When I arrived there, several days prior to the services, we were called into the KGB and the office of the local authorities. While sitting there, one of the men said to the local pastor, "It's wonderful that you have been able to renovate this building. And now you're going to hold gospel services in it. I forgot to tell you that it will cost you 100 percent duty for renovating the place. A dollar for dollar. It cost you eight thousand to renovate the place, so now it will cost you eight thousand dollars in taxes. You must bring that to us before you can have the first service. If you do not bring the eight thousand dollars, then you cannot open the door. I'm sorry, but otherwise we'll have to take it away from you—we'll have to confiscate it."

The pastor walked out of the building and I walked with him. As we arrived at his home, in the kitchen was his wife and another friend. Tearfully he told them the story as I sat there dumbfounded, wondering just what would take place. He turned to his wife and said, "We're going to pray and believe God for a miracle." Then the three of them knelt down by their little kitchen table and began talking to God like a child talking to his parents. They just simply opened their hearts to God and began to weep, saying, "Lord, you know, here we are in the midst of this country and no one really knows our need but You. Unless you help us, we will not have this building that we toiled so hard and worked so much for. We're looking forward to the day of the opening, and Pastor Derkatch is here with us, and we would have a glorious day, but Lord, if you don't send the eight thousand dollars we will not have the service or the building." Smiling, the pastor continued, "But dear Jesus, you will not disappoint us—You're going to send the eight thousand dollars!"

I heard it with my own ears and I cried! I was almost beside myself. I couldn't understand it all, but I knew that he touched heaven! They stood to their feet and then sat down, confident that all would be well. "God is going to supply our need!" he reassured me as they served a bit to eat. Then we praised God quietly before leaving for another service.

Ten days later, four days prior to the scheduled opening of that building for gospel services, a letter came by air mail with a little note in it stating that some ten days ago a lady in the United States—Missouri, to be exact—saw a vision at night. She saw the Soviet Bloc, and a man standing there. His need—eight thousand dollars! God spoke to her to send this man eight thousand dollars. The next morning she hurriedly mailed this eight thousand dollars to him, and it took ten days to get there. She also stated in her letter that she hoped she wasn't too late.

It was on time! This man and I walked to the same courtroom, meeting the same man that we did before, and with joy we handed him the eight thousand dollars. He looked at the money, and then at the pastor and myself, and then, turning back to the pastor, he said, "I don't believe in God, but there must be a higher source—somebody must have helped you! Who knew that you needed the money?"

That's the way God works! We have a wonderful Savior and God. Praise the Lord! We in the free countries must stand behind these people.

Another courier recently reported this experience. He had been invited to an underground church. This was a faithful church, for of the five hundred people present no one had spent less than three years in prison for his Christian faith, and one had spent 26 years. In his letter the courier wrote, "As we took the trolley and the bus and then the taxi, the KGB men were following us constantly. When we embarked on the bus the last time, just before we were to go up a hill for the service, and the KGB man was right behind me, I stood on the door until the bus was almost in motion and then jumped off, leaving him standing there. I walked to the pastor with a little smile and said, 'We lost him!' But the pastor said, 'Oh no we didn't; we lost *him*, but that Volga car was following us all the way! They know where we are going, but you get lost in the crowd and then go up the hill, as the cars can't go there.'

"While we were making our way up the hill, a brother came halfway down to warn us not to proceed any further, as the KGB men were there telling the people to disperse or be arrested. 'Please don't go!' he pleaded, and I looked at the pastor, who stood there for a moment and then said, 'No, we must go. We cannot betray our people; we cannot have them arrested with us looking on down here. We must stand by our people!' You can imagine how I felt.

"Up the hill we went, where I saw five hundred people, former imprisoned Christians, and they began to testify. These people, who had suffered so much, began thanking God for the privilege of suffering for Christ. They looked at me as though saying, 'What have you done for Christ? How much have you suffered for Him?' When they were all done testifying, they asked me to speak. Brother, what do you say to people who were in prison for three years, five years, ten years, and even more? What do you tell them? I first told them that I love Jesus, and they began to weep. I assured them that those in America and the Western world know all about them and their persecutions, and they continued weeping. I preached for half an hour, and the minute I stopped someone told us the KGB was there. As the news spread, some of those men simply would not allow the KGB men to come near us. They just surrounded the KGB men until the pastor and I went out of the crowd and came to a tall fence, which they heaved us over. Then we ran across the field, making our way toward the main street of the city. It seemed as if all the dogs in that town were barking at us, and the police on motorcycles were traveling fast and slow to try to apprehend us, but everytime a motorcycle came near us we fell flat on our faces in the tall grass and they couldn't find us.

"When we hit the main highway we went back to the hotel, and I began to praise God I was there. During our time with these faithful ones, the brethren told me this: 'Please do not write us off! Please remember us in your prayers and remember us in our plight. Remember our children. Please send us the tools. We are prepared to suffer and do all that God would ask us to do, but please send us the tools! Send us the Word of God! Send us paper! Send us gospel literature! Give us also the gospel program! Please do not write us off!'"

We thank God for the privilege that is ours to be able to send many hundreds and thousands of Russian, Ukrainian, and other nationality Bibles into these areas. If you were there with me and saw so many hundreds and thousands of boys and girls, young people and older people, all looking forward for the precious Word of God, your heart would be moved.

Chapter 14

Couriers

For thy word hath quickened me.
        —Psalm 119:50

We have some of the giants that God has on this earth as far as couriers are concerned. One of them is truly a great man of God.

When I wanted to meet with him I wrote him a letter from a certain country, but he did not receive it. When I arrived there I couldn't spot him at the airport. I knew he wasn't there, so I took a bus into the hotel and I looked around there, but still I couldn't see him. I booked in, had something to eat, and went to my room, where I prayed, "Lord, something has happened. There's no communication. He hasn't written. I wonder if he has received my letter? What has happened here?"

The next day I looked around again, but my friend still wasn't there. I took a bus and went on a tour, and then I thought, "Well, I have written him two letters telling him I would be here, and in the second letter that I'm going to be in Vienna also." So the next day I went over to the counter and said, "Now look, I don't feel too good, and I'd like to fly out to Vienna." They said, "Fine, that could be arranged." So I took the first flight out.

While I was in Vienna a letter came from the courier saying, "Brother, I received your letter.

You're going to be in Vienna. I'm looking forward to your being in my country. I want to have time to talk with you." I thought, "Lord, I was just there; he didn't receive the letter I wrote telling him I was going to be there." So I prayed again, "Lord, help me to get back to that country. And help me to meet with this brother because it is so important to do so before my mission is completed."

I went back to the consulate, where I met with the ambassador. I told him I had been in his country just a couple of days ago and had left because I was sick. "Now I feel all right," I continued, "and I'd like to go back and complete my mission there. My tour is in there, and I still have three days of visa. Would you still honor them?" He looked at my papers and then replied, "I think so."

"How long before I could leave?"

"Whenever you want to."

"In two days' time?"

"Fine."

I went to the telegraph office and asked how long it took for a telegram to reach a certain place, and they told me half an hour. So I wrote a brief note to that brother: "Arriving at the airport on flight so and so at five P.M." The next day I was on the scheduled flight out.

About eight o'clock that night someone told me there was a person to see me. I had never met this brother before, although we were corresponding and he was our courier for a long time. I came down and saw this handsome, dark, curly-haired fellow standing by the counter. I walked close to him and greeted him and he showed me my picture. I wondered who had given him my picture, and he turned it around and showed me the man's name. That was fine, so I pulled out his picture from my pocket and gave it to him, showing the name, and he said, "That's fine."

We talked for about five minutes and walked outside for another five minutes, and then I said, "Look, all eyes are upon us, so you must disappear. Don't come back tomorrow, but come back the day after."

"Fine, I'll meet you in two days."

The next day I got up early in the morning, had a good breakfast, and then asked the lady at the counter how many tours they had.

"Three tours—one in the morning, one after dinner, and one at night."

"Wonderful, I want the three tours all in one day!"

"Great."

So they gave me three tickets, and let me assure you, I made some tours and did some sightseeing during that whole day. I wanted to impress them that I was there as a tourist, and I did just that!

The next day I went back to the same counter, where I said to the lady, "You know, yesterday those tours took much out of me, so today I want to relax, to just go out and walk around."

"Fine, you did wonderfully well yesterday."

"That's good; thank you."

I walked outside and met my man about two blocks from the hotel. He was wearing a little country hat and had another one in his pocket, which he gave me to wear. We hailed a taxi and, with these hats on our heads, we got in.

"Where do you want to go?" the driver asked.

"As far as you want to take us this way," my man replied.

We drove seven miles from the hotel, almost out of the city limits. Then we disembarked to walk the seven miles back. As we walked, we planned our tours and how to smuggle Bibles into the different areas, and we talked about our brethren.

"If I could only own a car," he said. "I know how I could manipulate to buy one here, but it would cost me twelve hundred dollars. I can promise you that with it I would take five hundred Bibles into the Soviet Union every month."

"Brother," I said, "that's very dangerous. Where is the car?" He said, "Let's take a taxi and we'll go this way, and when we arrive there you'll speak to the man in the English language while I wait outside. I do not understand the English language, but you ask me questions to which I will say "yes" twice and "no" once, and this will impress him that I know the English language."

Doing just that, the man suggested that we go and look at the cars, so we went a little further and looked at them. My courier said, "This is the car I want," pointing to a small European vehicle. We made the arrangements to supply him with it, and in the next four years he brought over 24,000 Bibles into the Soviet Bloc, and our only transportation cost was twelve hundred dollars!

While we were talking about his plans and the border crossing he would be using, I said, "Brother, that's a very dangerous crossing. You are in great danger!"

"I know," he replied. "I am 52 years of age and I have spent 25 years of my life in the Russian prison. I know the Russian prison. Do you see the scars on my face?"

"I certainly do."

"I received them in those prisons, and I wouldn't want to go back to those jails, but if God wants me to, I will. Brother, you saw the need, and you know how great it is. Not only that, but if God wants me to, I am not only willing to go to jail for Him and my brethren, but I am willing to die for Him!"

We were already walking back to my hotel when he said those words. This was after we had spent over six hours making plans and contacts for this dangerous mission. His last words were that he was willing and ready to die for God! These are the kinds of couriers God has given World Christian Ministries, and we praise God we can take hundreds of thousands of Bibles behind the Iron Curtain even now!

Here is a description of an incident that another of our couriers experienced. "Clear directions were given, as I expressed my concern about families with someone in prison. I was sent to the home of a woman in tremendous need, for her husband was serving time for refusing to denounce his commitment to Jesus Christ. I had to go alone, with only instructions I had memorized from the pastor.

"On the bus I became conscious that someone might be following, so I continued on an extra stop and walked back. Carefully I checked every corner, and finally I was able to evade my pursuer. Reaching the number I sought, I opened the gate and went directly to the back door. A young girl answered and then disappeared back into the house again, closing the door behind her. In a moment or so an older woman appeared and invited me onto the porch so that she could close the door and talk to me. Explaining to her who I was, where I was from and, why I was there, I realized we were getting nowhere, for she didn't believe a word I said.

"An older daughter joined us on the porch and began asking me questions. I showed her my passport and explained that I was a Christian who had come to help them. Finally, when they discovered we knew the same family in the United States, they believed me and took me into their living room.

"We started discussing plans of how to assist them when a knock came on the door. Fearing the police, they quickly closed the door of the room we were in and went to answer. Sitting alone, thoughts raced through my mind. . . . Had my pursuer succeeded in following me to this place? Was I noticed as I approached this home? Maybe a nosy neighbor saw our conversation at the back door and called the authorities. Then the door burst open and a large man came in. Looking straight at me, he extended his hand and said, 'Praise the Lord, Brother. I'm so happy to see you. Word has reached me of your work, and you have nothing to fear.' Relieved, we sat down and he joined us in the plans we were to make.

"To avoid suspicion, we agreed to meet again the next day, when he would bring several other believers along. The money would be divided among them to purchase necessary things for the needy. This way no one person would be making a large purchase, thereby creating suspicion, yet much could be obtained and put to use.

"The following morning I took his group to a store, and one by one they came in and began buying suits, coats, dresses, sweaters, watches, etc. I couldn't help but notice one man who bought about twenty fur hats at a certain price. Being rather shocked at what I considered an extravagance, I questioned him, saying that in America we could not afford to pay that much for a hat. 'Brother,' he said, 'as soon as the cold weather comes we will be able to sell these hats for about eight times that price. This is a sound investment, for it makes this money work even farther for us. There is no doubt this is one of the best buys we can make.' This man had foresight I could not have had, and they were making the best possible purchases with the money I had given them. As the shopping spree concluded, a person with his parcels would disappear in one direction while another with more parcels would go in another. Soon I was left alone and the parcels were all gone, but I knew that though my purse was empty many were going to benefit from it and that a great mission had been completed for the day."

Chapter 15

Just for a Bible

He shall give thee the desires of thine heart.

—Psalm 37:4

There is nothing more precious to a Russian believer than to own a Bible. We were in a service in one of the major cities of the Communist Bloc. As it drew to a close a lady edged her way forward, and when she got near me she asked, "Do you have a Bible?"

I said, "No."

"Do you have any gospel literature?"

"Really, no."

"Don't you have anything at all?"

I thought for a moment or so before I replied. "Well, I do have four little booklets, but they're all spoken for."

"You mean, then, that you really do have some printed gospel material?"

"Yes, I guess I do."

"Would I ever appreciate having them."

"But I told you, they're all spoken for!"

"Could I at least see them?"

"They're in my hotel room, and it's at least three miles from here."

"That's fine—my husband and I and our two little girls will walk with you to the hotel room. I want to see those booklets."

I tried to brush her off but I couldn't. They just insisted on going with me to the hotel.

When we arrived, we walked up three flights of stairs, then went down the long hall to my room. Inside, I pulled from my briefcase the four little booklets. They were very thin, and tears came to her eyes as she took them. She read one paragraph, then she said to me, "May I have this booklet?"

"No, Sister, it's already spoken for. I really can't give it to you."

"Please, may I have it?"

"But it's already spoken for. I want to give it to a brother in another city about a thousand miles away from here. I'm going that way and he'll be disappointed if I don't have it. Sister, I just can't give it to you."

"But in Jesus' name, don't take it away from me!"

"Fine, you can have it."

When she heard that, she put the little booklet between the palms of her hands and prayed these words: "Dear Jesus, I thank you for this precious little booklet, this precious gift, the most wonderful gift that I have received in the last 25 years. I thank you for this man who brought it to me this afternoon."

With tears coursing down her eyes she turned around, and with her husband and the two girls she left the room and went down the three flights of stairs. I watched them from the window as they made their way to the subway. Then I fell on my bed, buried my head in my pillow in the deep of Russia, and wept like a little baby. I said,

"Dear Lord, that little booklet in our land is not worth more than 25 cents. This lady has told you that this little booklet was so precious in her sight, the best gift she has received in the past 25 years. She wasn't talking to me, she was talking to You, Lord. Help us, help our brethren in America, Canada, and the Western world to share what we have so that we can give these precious Bibles to those that are so hungry for them."

In another place where I was preaching, an older man was sitting beside me. He turned to me and said, "Brother, for 45 years I have been preaching the gospel in the Soviet Union and I don't own a Bible. The brother next to you has a full Bible. Would you ask him to share his with me, to give me at least half of his?"

The brother overheard and said, "No, not the Bible. I'll give him anything I have, but not the Bible." I have seen people walk fifty miles just to be able to read a Bible and hold one in their hands. I know a minister who walked 28 miles to marry a couple, and he needed a Bible. They wanted to have a Christian wedding, but the minister did not have a Bible. He walked seven miles to borrow a Bible from his friend, who said, "No, I won't give you my Bible; you'll never return it." The preacher said, "I promise you before God that I'll bring it back."

"If you promise before God, then I'll loan it to you, but you must return it to me immediately."

He then walked seven miles to marry the couple, seven miles back to his friend, and then the other seven miles home. Twenty-eight miles just to be able to read the Bible!

Chapter 16

The Weight
Of the Cross

*Whosoever will come after me, let him
deny himself and take up his cross and
follow me.*

—Mark 8:34

In one of my meetings a young man of about thirty approached me and said, "Friend of mine, how happy I am to be a Christian, to be born again, to know that Jesus Christ lives in my heart. Even though it cost me much, including my job and my future here in the homeland, I do thank God for this great plan of salvation. I was a radio navigator in our air force. I had plenty of money and a good position. My family was well secure. One day I turned on the radio and came across a Christian radio program. As we were flying across our country, I listened to this program and got great conviction about my sins. Jesus Christ began to speak to my heart, and before I brought that plane to a landing I was fully converted! I accepted Jesus Christ as my personal savior up there in the air!

"A few moments after we landed, I went and told my officer what had taken place, how Jesus Christ came into my heart, and how I had become a Christian. The officer looked at me and said, 'John, you're making a great mistake. If you continue this way, we will have to discharge you. We will have to give you a dishonorable discharge. You will lose your security, you will lose your job, you will be punished, and your children and wife will starve. Why are you so foolish? You must reject this Christianity and deny God! You know that we're against it!' But I had to look him straight in the face and tell him that Jesus has done much more for me right now than my job on earth, and I will never be able to reject Jesus Christ as my own personal Savior!"

Continuing with his story, he told me they took him into a large office, where, after several minutes of interrogation, they beat him up and knocked him unconscious. Then they poured cold water on him to bring him to and asked him again if he would deny God and reject Jesus Christ. "I cannot deny God, I cannot reject Jesus Christ!" he told them as they continued with their persecution. Finally he blacked out, and during this time God gave him a vision. "I saw the Lord Jesus Christ, and I saw Him so beautifully as He said to me, 'John, I have been persecuted for you, I have been molested for you, and I have died for you. Will you not suffer for me now?' I shouted aloud, 'Yes, Jesus Christ, I am prepared to suffer and die for You, and I thank you for this great salvation, for saving my never-dying soul!'

"In the meantime a few of the officers went to my home and began telling my wife what happened to me, how I was now a Christian and how foolish I was because I was going to lose all that I had, and how the children and she would suffer if she didn't insist that I reject the Lord Jesus Christ. My wife told the officers that she was not

143

ashamed of me, that she knew the stand that I had taken and that she was a Christian also. 'If you take everything away from us here,' she told them, 'we will still have a beautiful home in heaven.' The officers then left, returning to the prison, where they continued to beat me before throwing me into prison, where I stayed for a long period of time."

They took the beautiful living quarters away from his family and put them into a one-room place with no windows and only a trap door to enter. "We lost everything but that one room," he continued, "but I know that in heaven we'll have a great room with plenty of windows."

After they released him, for some six months they would not allow him to get a job. He would go from place to place picking up odd jobs here and there and living very meagerly, but he was contented, for now they were saved. That is not the end of his story, for I am happy to tell you that he is still a very fervent preacher of the gospel of Jesus Christ and is busy in the Soviet Bloc, preaching and sharing the good news with others.

No, there is not religious liberty behind the Iron Curtain, and those who think there is are being deceived by the masters of deceit. A great price is paid by the Christians to worship the Living God, and they are constantly looking to us for our prayers and help.

My many months in these countries have brought continued confirmation of the great need for the printed Word of God and other Christian literature. I have faced grown men who tearfully

144

begged me for Bibles and other Christian literature. They've assured me they were willing to go
to great risk to obtain it. We at home have such a
responsibility! Only together can we carry it out!

Chapter 17

From Here On

*Unto whomsoever much is given, of
him shall be much required.*
—Luke 12:48

I was quickly brought back to the present by the jingling of my telephone. The call was from overseas, and the caller, Brother X, was another one of our couriers. Throughout my years of traveling, I made contact with people willing to become couriers and take these great risks to bring God's Word to people behind the Iron Curtain. To many I assigned part-time jobs of carrying literature, while others have been asked to be on the alert for new openings and ways of getting the Word in.

Brother X was excited as he talked to me. For several months now the Christians had been observing a certain area and the habits of the guards along the border there. Also, they made contact with Christians within and found that few Bibles existed among the believers. There was a great need, and now an effective chain of dedicated people was ready to go.

World Christian Ministries was to swing into action again in another area. The demand was for five hundred Bibles a day, and they were sure they could use this plan for several months before changing it.

I scanned our present commitments as I talked with Brother X. It would be "nip and tuck" as to whether we could meet this demand. All of our costs here at home are skyrocketing and money is scarce, but we would certainly try. Then a fearful thought raced through my mind. "What if we had to say 'no' to some of these people?" What if they needed God's word, and we as their privileged brothers could not send it to them? What if World Christian Ministries could no longer function? What a terrible thing that would be!

But then the Lord assured me that this would not happen. Over the years He pointed out how He had raised up this organization to meet the tremendous need. It was nothing short of a miracle how He sent me there in the first place and then provided, here in Canada and the United States, the resources to get the Bibles and literature printed. Every door that opened and every courier made available was a miracle also, for each person is a specialist in his own right.

The effect of World Christian Ministries has reached into almost every Curtained country in the world, and many have been saved and are growing for Christ today because of WCM. But it is a work that involves and needs us all. We cannot supply our couriers unless we have finances to provide the printed materials. You cannot do a proper job with financial assistance unless you know that you have a reliable place to put it, a place where there are experienced people doing the job. Our faithfulness all around is so important.

I am reminded of an incident I experienced behind the Iron Curtain. The Communists are very loyal to their country. One late night, after a lengthy gospel service, I arrived back at my hotel to find the dining hall packed with a banquet in progress. There was no room for anyone else to enter. It was rather late at night, and they were not serving anyone else. I turned around and went to the counter to ask the clerk if I could have something to eat, explaining that I was hungry and had just arrived. They prepared a meal for me in one of their offices, and during the course of being served I asked the lady how her family was, how she enjoyed her job, etc.

She told me she had been married for one year and that her husband now had to go to the army, where she would not see him for three years or possibly even five years, depending on the condition of the world. Continuing her conversation, she said, "We here in our land put our country ahead of our own personal desires and needs. After I was married I had to accept the idea that if he was to leave for any length of time up to five years, I would be glad to see him go. I hear from him periodically, but I will not see him for three years. We were only married for one year."

I thought to myself, "My God, here is a lady who does not know God or her future and yet is so devoted to her country. How much more we as Christians ought to be devoted and pay allegiance to our heavenly country, for the Christ who died that you and I might have everlasting life."

When we see devotion like this, it is enough to make many of us Christians ashamed. We hesitate to talk about Jesus to others because we wonder what they might think, and yet there are those who allow themselves to be deprived of normal life just to serve their country. We can certainly learn from these people, and if I could take you with me to see the dedication of the Iron Curtain Christians, you would be challenged even more.

Amidst the severe persecution being meted out to believers, there are stalwart Christians who are daily obeying the the Lord's command instead of their own government's wishes. They believe the Bible when it says, "Go ye into all the world and preach the gospel to every creature."

We must continue to supply them with the necessary tools to do the job. These tools include your prayers and financial assistance. World Christian Ministries has the responsibility of providing printed materials, transportation, radio broadcasts, and financial assistance to the Iron Curtain countries.

I wonder, when you go to bed tonight, whether you will be thinking of the Christian who is in a dark, damp cell somewhere because he was willing to serve Jesus. Will you remember his family, who can't get a job because Dad is a Christian? Will you pray for those who are saying to us "Don't write us off! Send us your prayers and send us the Bible! Help us to share God among our nations!"

You have just been reading the World Christian Ministries story, and how God built it over the years. There is no way that I as its founder, or even my late brother Michael, would want to take any credit for it. God has raised it up, and

He is expecting that hearts will be moved by the need and that many will continue to support World Christian Mission Ministries. The story *must* continue and *will* continue as long as there is a need. If you believe in this ministry, I pray that you will support it with your prayers and assistance.

Perhaps, as you have read this book, you realize that you have never experienced Jesus Christ in a living way in your life, that you have never accepted Jesus Christ as your personal Savior. As you read of the changing power Jesus gives our persecuted believers behind the Iron Curtain, you know that this is what you want also.

Friend, the way to God is simple—it is through Jesus Christ. According to John 14:6, He is the only way. When we realize our need of God, we also realize that we are sinners, that is, that our life has sin in it. Then we need only turn to Jesus Christ, for God sent Him to pay for our sins. God is the same today as always. Even as His power lifted Jesus from the tomb, so we can now have that same power enter into our lives. But we must call on Him and ask him in today. Each one who does this has to do it personally, asking Christ into his own heart. I trust that you will do so, thereby joining the ranks of millions who now know God in a personal way.

Then I hope you will join with many who are praying for World Christian Ministries, and the thousands of people we reach through God's help each year. With the help of God, this work shall go on, for there are no boundaries with God!

After reading this book, perhaps your interest has been stirred for our suffering brethren overseas. World Christian Ministries is working with these people on a consistent basis, and we solicit your prayers and support. For further information or for additional copies of this book, write:

WORLD   CHRISTIAN   MINISTRIES
Box 405, Station D, Toronto, Ontario M6P 3J9 Canada
or
P.O. Box 2010, Orange, California 92669 U.S.A.

OUR MINISTRY TO THE IRON CURTAIN

Radio

Aiding Established Ministries

Aiding Orphans & the Poor

Gospel Records

Gospel Outreach

Clothes

Bibles

Gospel Helps (Hymnals, Concordances, etc)

GIVING LIGHT TO EASTERN EUROPE

* **RADIO** — Broadcasting the gospel into the U.S.S.R.
* **BIBLES** — Sending Bibles into Russia, the Ukraine, and Communist-dominated countries
* **GOSPEL RECORDS** — Sending Slavic gospel albums into the U.S.S.R.
* **GOSPEL LITERATURE** — Reaching behind the Iron Curtain with concordances, youth materials, tracts, hymnals, etc.
* **AIDING ORPHANS** — Helping the underprivileged, orphans, and families with imprisoned or martyred families
* **CLOTHING** — Supplying the poor and underprivileged brethren in Christ with essential clothing
* **AIDING MINISTRIES** — Supporting our brethren in eastern Europe to help spread the gospel
* **CONTEMPORARY OUTREACH** — Meeting the Need of the Hour

WORLD CHRISTIAN MINISTRIES
Box 405, Station D, Toronto, Ontario M6P 3J9 Canada

World Christian Ministries is well known to the Canadian Bible Society, and its work of providing the Word of God for people in desperate need of spiritual comfort is followed with close interest.

The Canadian Bible Society does all that it can to help by providing Scriptures at as reasonable a cost as possible in order that the funds raised by World Christian Ministries shall provide the utmost quantity of the Scriptures.

K. Rhodes
Secretary & Business Manager
Canadian Bible Society
Toronto

Having been in the Soviet Union, I know that the need for Bibles is very real. I have personally watched the printing of Bibles for World Christian Ministries destined for Iron Curtain countries.

I have every confidence that World Christian Ministries is very effective and most efficient in supplying Bibles and other Christian literature to the Communist countries.

David Mainse
Host and Executive Producer
Crossroads Telecast